Country Collections

TIME-LIFE BOOKS

Alexandria, Virginia

Country Collections

*ideas for collecting
and displaying antiques and
other country treasures*

A REBUS BOOK

C O N T E N T S

Personal Effects

Collectors' Choice

W hether you are interested in kitchen utensils, tableware, antique tools, or vintage linens, assembling a collection is a process of discovery. For many collectors, the pursuit of the right piece—and the friendships and knowledge that are frequently gained along the way—brings as much pleasure as the actual find.

There are many ways to start collecting. Some people take a deliberate approach, beginning with a careful study of whatever subject interests them, then progressing to a well-informed search for collectibles that relate to it. Others are inspired to build a collection around a family heirloom or a chance find at a flea market. Often, collections are well under way before people even realize they have become collectors. Someone who enjoys sewing, for instance, might be naturally attracted to early needlework tools, and make an occasional purchase at antiques shops and shows. At some point, however, a particularly intriguing sewing box, perhaps, or an interesting conversation with a dealer will pique a buyer's interest, and casual curiosity will turn into serious pursuit. Then the real thrill of collecting begins.

Reading, visiting museums, joining clubs and associations for collectors, and frequenting auctions and fairs are all good ways to develop expertise. Learning when and where objects were made, how they were used, and why they were decorated in a particular fashion helps make a collection come alive. The more you study, examine objects in person, and compare prices, the better able you will be to judge quality and workmanship when you are considering a purchase.

Developing a solid understanding of a subject will also help to define the scope of a collection. The interest generated by reading might prompt the collector of needlework, for example, to focus solely on thimbles, or to specialize in Victorian sewing implements. On the other hand, an individual may decide that gathering a cross section of tools—such as scissors, pincushions, and needlecases that date from two or three centuries—is the most satisfying way to proceed.

A sampler of American country collections, this volume reveals that collecting—whether it is a casual pastime or a consuming passion—has no set rules. The objects shown in the following chapters, including household goods, kitchen utensils, dinnerware, and clothing and other personal effects, range from the commonplace to the unexpected and illustrate some of the many ways a collection can be developed and displayed. You will find that people have their own ideas of what makes a thought-provoking and attractive collection, and of how much time, energy, and household space they want to devote to it. Ultimately, the best collections reflect the personality and enthusiasm of the collectors themselves.

Around the House

practical tools and accessories
from America's past

The chores required for running an efficient household used to be so numerous and time-consuming that certain days were customarily set aside for certain tasks. A 19th-century housewife had the following maxim to go by: "Wash on Monday, iron on Tuesday, bake on Wednesday, brew on Thursday, churn on Friday, mend on Saturday, and go to church on Sunday."

From laundry equipment to lanterns, the implements that were once associated with everyday life around the house are now popular collectibles. As this chapter shows, even the most utilitarian household object is likely to catch a collector's eye. Some, like buttons and doorstops, are attractive for the sense of humor or whimsy that they convey. Others, such as a mirror-backed sconce or a tin candle mold, are appealing because of their clever designs adapted to specific needs. Intriguing reminders of the past, such collectibles are a welcome addition to country homes.

Victorian pincushions often took the form of fruits and vegetables.

Painted Baskets

Painted splint baskets like the 19th-century pieces shown here are a specialty among basket collectors. Woven from thin strips of ash, oak, or hickory, splint baskets themselves were among the most widely produced American basket types in the 1800s. Used for ordinary tasks like gathering potatoes, they were generally left plain. When paint was added, it provided more than color; it also afforded protection against dampness and wear.

The same kind of paint that was used on furniture was also suitable for baskets. It was usually made from powdered pigments mixed with oil or buttermilk; commercially made paint did not become available until the turn of the century. The rarest basket color is yellow, while green and red are seen most often. Blue is also common, but because this color is now so popular, it can raise the price of an antique basket.

Baskets were often repainted and some reveal several layers of color built up over many years. Original paint will show signs of wear on the handles and rims and in places where the bottom of the basket rests on a surface.

Because baskets were generally discarded when they wore out, few examples found today date from earlier than the mid-1800s. The most common are round or rectangular in shape with flat bottoms and stationary handles. Collectors look for pieces with unusual forms, like the distinctive apple-picking basket on the floor at right, whose indented side was designed to fit on the hip. The wooden swivel handles on some of the baskets above are another sign of value. Such baskets are finds in themselves; colored with their original paint, they are true prizes.

If it is original, the paint on early baskets like the 19th-century pieces above and at right will show signs of wear. The paint on large farm baskets is likely to be more worn than that on small tabletop baskets.

Indian Baskets

Most of the American Indian baskets collected today date from the 1800s or early 1900s, when such baskets were woven for sale to traders and tourists. Coiled baskets, like those opposite crafted by the Apache, Pima, and Mission tribes, were found throughout the Southwest. These baskets were made by stitching together coiled bundles of plant materials—usually pine needles, grass, or leaves—with dyed grasses. Black and red dyes from plants were used for early baskets, but by the end of the 1800s, bright aniline colors were common. Certain basket shapes are characteristic of particular tribes: the ollas, or jar forms, for example, were Apache designs, while low,

small-necked bowls were crafted by California Mission Indians.

Covered splint baskets like those above were the work of northeastern Algonquian and Iroquois Indians, who may have learned the craft from European settlers. Prior to 1880, most Indian baskets from the Northeast had broad splints—about an inch wide—that lent themselves to bold decoration. Floral motifs were common, and they varied depending on where the baskets were made. In Connecticut, the Mohegan shaped flowers with dots, while graphic floral repeat patterns applied with potato stamps are typical of baskets made by tribes in northern New England and New York.

The decorated splint baskets above were made by Algonquian and Iroquois Indians in the northeastern United States. If the dyed decorations that are characteristic of such baskets are original, they will usually look transparent and naturally faded.

The coiled baskets opposite show designs typical of certain tribes. The Apache favored figures, the Pima made mazelike designs, and the Mission Indians used diamond and stepped patterns.

Nantucket Lightship Baskets

Tightly woven rattan baskets made with sturdy wooden bottoms have long been associated with the South Shoal Lightship, anchored off Nantucket Island, Massachusetts, from 1856 into the 1900s. Essentially a floating lighthouse, this 103-foot-long schooner was home to a ten-man crew on an eight-month rotation. During those lonely months, the men stood watch, operated and maintained the ship's two powerful beacons, and—as a primary source of recreation—made baskets that were later sold on shore.

Such baskets, originally known simply as rattan baskets, were in fact woven as early as the 1820s by Nantucket residents, who used buckets and other rounded objects as molds. When the craft proved a profitable and practical means for the lightship crewmen to while away the hours, the basketmaking was transferred largely to the ship. The name "lightship basket," however, came to refer to any molded rattan basket with a wooden bottom, including those that had actually been made on shore.

The lightship crewmen usually made nesting sets of five to eight baskets in sizes ranging from about a pint to a peck and a half (twelve quarts). They wove them according to the traditional Nantucket method, using special wooden molds—both round and oval—taken aboard the lightship during its first year of operation. To begin, the mold was affixed to a wooden base that had also been made on the island. Next, ribs made of oak or hickory were fitted into a quarter-inch groove running around the edge of the base. The ribs were then sponged down with boiling water to make them pliable, and tied around the mold with a cord. A day later, the men would untie the ribs, remove the mold, and begin weaving in the rattan. When the weaving was done, a rim was made from two slender, half-round hoops of oak whipped together with rattan. Finally, oak handles were added.

Around 1905, the last of the basketmaking crewmen left the lightship, and the craft of basketmaking returned to the island with them: ashore, the former crewmen and other craftsmen carried on the tradition, which continues today. While many of the early makers remain anonymous, some, like W. M. Gibbs, A. D. Williams, and Mitchell Ray, labeled their finely made baskets and are well-known. Ray, who was a third-generation basketmaker, often included the following rhyme on his label: "I was made on Nantucket, I'm strong and I'm stout. Don't lose me or burn me, and I'll never wear out."

The Nantucket lightship baskets at right date from the 1890s to the 1940s and are typical of the sturdy rattan baskets made aboard the South Shoal Lightship and on the island itself.

Early Candle-holders

Typical of pieces used in public buildings, the tin candelabra at right include, clockwise from upper left, an 1850s triangular stand thought to be a Masonic design; a graceful 1820s piece made in New England; an 1840s five-socket candelabra; a twelve-candle light from the early 19th century; and an adjustable double candlestick (this is the only one that might have been used in a house).

Throughout the 18th and 19th centuries, a variety of inexpensive candleholders could be found in most American households. The 19th-century hogscraper candlesticks above—so called because they resembled a tool used for scraping bristles off hides—were among the most common types. Most of the hogscraper candlesticks shown here were imported in quantity from England; the best pieces were trimmed with a decorative brass or iron ring and might have a sliding "ejector," which was used to push up the candle as it burned. Hogscrapers were typically made of iron or tin.

What was called tin, however, was actually sheet iron plated with tin to protect against rust. Although this "tin" lacked the rich patina of silver, its reflective surface glittered impressively in candlelight, and the material was sometimes used for candelabra like the 19th-century pieces at left. Intended for churches and other public buildings, candelabra were never widely produced for common household use because it was too expensive to supply them with candles.

Some of the hogscraper candlesticks above were made with a hook, or "spur," on the upper rim.
Such candlesticks were designed so that they could be hung from the top slat of ladder-back chairs
to serve as reading lamps.

Candle Equipment

Lighting a house with candles in 18th- and 19th- century America was a time-consuming task. Special equipment was required not only for producing candles, but also for trimming and storing them.

In early years, candles were made by dipping wicks in hot wax. From the late 18th century onward, however, the availability of molds simplified candlemaking. Molds were typically crafted in tin or pewter; rare types include earthenware-and-wood molds made during the 19th century.

While some candles were made of beeswax or the wax from bayberries, most were of tallow, or rendered animal fat. Tallow candles were especially vulnerable to damage because the fat

attracted rodents; moreover, the candles were apt to become soft in a warm room. Consequently, candles were usually stored in a large box with a sliding lid. As the candles were needed, they were moved to a smaller wall box with a hinged lid. Collectors look for boxes with grain-painting, stenciling, or carving.

Additional tools were necessary to keep the household supply of candles in good condition. Conical-shaped snuffers extinguished the flame without bending the wick or spattering wax. Scissorlike snuffers were used to put out the candle and to trim the wick: a small box or tray at the tip caught the cut-off portion. Typically made of iron, tin, or brass, snuffers can sometimes be found with a matching tray.

The collection above includes candles, storage boxes—the largest holds several dozen candles—and various snuffers, all from the 18th and 19th centuries.

DECORATIVE CANDLES

The simple act of lighting a few candles can transform the mood of a room in an instant. Indeed, candles are an effective decorating accent, and their look can be as distinctive as that of the candleholder itself.

At left are some of the many styles and types of candles available today. These include molded votive and pillar candles, as well as hand-dipped candles, which have a handsome country look and are available in a wide variety of sizes and colors.

A favorite is the bayberry candle—made with wax from bayberries—which has been valued for its even burning and its fresh scent since colonial times. One old New England rhyme claims:

> *A bayberry candle burned in the socket*
> *Brings health to the home and gold to the pocket.*

Another traditional candle type is the beeswax candle, hand-rolled from sheets of honeycomb. These unusual candles burn without dripping and emit a delicate fragrance of honey. As the candle burns down, the flame softly illuminates the honeycomb pattern.

Available from specialty shops, the decorative candles at left include hand-dipped tapers; beeswax candles; votives, nesting in tiny muffin tins; and stocky pillar candles.

The 18th- and 19th-century sconces at right are made of tin; when new, the metal had a shiny, reflective surface. Mirrored sconces with their original glass intact are sought-after today, as are the rare sconces designed to hold more than one candle. The sconce made with a reflective back of glass prisms and balls, top row, and the three-candle sconce, bottom row, are prized pieces in this collection.

Used in houses throughout the 18th and 19th centuries, sconces were designed to magnify candlelight by reflecting it into a room. Although these decorative wall brackets were made in brass and silver, which could be rubbed to a bright finish, less costly tin sconces, like those above, were more common.

The simple sconces found in houses were sometimes hammered or scored to create convex patterns and facets that imitated the look of mirror pieces and also helped their ability to reflect light. More elaborate tin sconces were actually

Tin Sconces

lined with beveled glass or pieces of mirror, and were typically used in taverns and other public buildings; their greater reflecting power was advantageous in lighting large rooms.

Sconce design tended to follow the prevailing furniture styles. During the late 1700s, for instance, sconce backs might be made in a rounded fan shape, a popular decorative motif at the time. During the Federal period in the early 1800s, when classically inspired designs and geometric silhouettes were favored, sconces were made in oval and rectangular shapes.

Candle Lanterns

The tin and wood lanterns at right date from the 18th and 19th centuries. The pierced-tin lanterns are sometimes called Paul Revere lanterns, but they actually emit far too little light to be an effective beacon. Lanterns that hold more than one candle are extremely rare.

Candle lanterns like the 18th- and 19th-century examples above were simple devices designed to shield the flame from drafts and make candles safer to carry while lit. Until the late 1800s, such lanterns were typically hung by entryways or carried outdoors.

Pierced-tin lanterns emitted very little light but were inexpensive and thus quite common. Collectors look for pierced patterns based on patriotic or Masonic motifs, and unusual forms such as those with bull's-eye windows.

Another basic type of candle lantern is characterized by a tin or wood frame and glass-paneled sides—one of which opens. On some examples thin horn was used instead of glass, and these lanterns are considered rare finds.

Light and Interiors

The practice of arranging a room according to personal preference is a relatively recent development. Until the mid-1800s the placement of furnishings was not a matter of taste, but was instead dictated by the availability of natural and artificial light.

Until the end of the 18th century, furniture was typically lined up along the walls of a room and moved to a suitable spot when needed. During the day, for example, chairs used for sewing or reading would be carried from one window to another as the sun shifted from east to west. After dark, a table was pulled out and set with candles for dining, and a chair and workstand might be drawn up to the light of the fire. Because furniture was moved so frequently, decorative objects had no place on tabletops; instead they were displayed on mantels or walls.

A breakthrough in lighting technology occurred in 1783, when a Swiss chemist named Aimé Argand developed a smokeless oil burner that generated a light equal in strength to the glow of about ten candles. With the Argand burner, evening light became more stationary.

Because the burners were cumbersome and were moved only when necessary, a piece of furniture—a sofa perhaps—might be positioned near the light and left in place. This marked the beginning of the idea of a fixed furniture arrangement.

Further changes occurred during the 1830s and 1840s, when the Astral oil lamp became available. With the Astral lamp came the center table, designed specifically to make maxi-use of the lamp's shadowless light; usually, the table was round, as was the fall of light from the lamp. Chairs could be drawn up around the table for tea, games, or family discussions. At the end of an evening, the chairs were put back along a wall, but the table, with its lamp, remained a fixture in the center of the room.

Not until the mid-1800s and the arrival of gas lamps, which were mounted on walls or hung as chandeliers, did room arrangements become more elaborate. Chairs, sofas, and tables began to be clustered in small groupings under the circular fall of lamplight. It was then that set furniture arrangements became the rule rather than the exception.

Oil-Burning Lamps

I n America, the use of oil lamps—which were common in most households from the 17th century to the mid-1800s—paralleled that of candles. One of the simplest types was the betty lamp, which burned fish oil or grease. The exact origin of the name is unknown, but it may be a corruption of the word "better." While they were sooty and smelly, and produced a very dim light, betty lamps like those at top right were an improvement over earlier grease lamps, in which a rag wick sat in a pan of fuel. Made of tin or cast iron, betty lamps had hinged lids, which reduced the possibility of the wick igniting the oil, and iron channels, which kept the wick from dripping the oil. They usually included a hook for hanging, and a pick for adjusting the wick.

Whale oil—in general use by 1760—came as a welcome alternative to grease because it burned with a clean, odorless flame. People on both sides of the Atlantic had tried to tap its potential as lamp fuel since the beginning of the century. Finally, an Englishman named John Miles introduced a whale-oil burner with a vertical wick that rose from an enclosed oil reservoir, which prevented the valuable oil from spilling.

Miles's innovative lamp inspired dozens of American variations. Based on his vertical-wick design, the 19th-century lamps at bottom right combine free-blown glass globes with tin chimneys. The large one shown here is the biggest

Betty lamps, above, were made in America from the 1600s until the mid-19th century. The onion lanterns, right, date from about 1830 to 1850.

of its type known to have been made; the red glass example was probably a signal lamp. Known as onion lanterns, such pieces are rare because so many have broken.

More commonly found variations on the Miles lamp include tin pieces like the whale-oil lamps at top left. The three-burner pig lamp—named for its porcine appearance—in the center of the top shelf was also known as a guest room lamp; the spherical example to its left is an American copy of John Miles's original design.

Many collectors of early oil lamps try to find one of each type; patent lamps, like those at bottom left, offer a considerable challenge. In the mid-1800s, the rising cost of whale oil promoted experimentation with other fuels, particularly lard oil and camphene (a mixture of lard oil and turpentine). As a result, hundreds of individuals rushed to invent and patent lamps that would burn these fuels efficiently: each design was different from the others. The patent lamps shown here include two police lamps on the top shelf, designed with bull's-eye lenses that could be covered for stealth. The shaded lamp burned lard.

Most of the patents on such lamps were taken out between 1850 and the 1860s, when kerosene became available. The lamps are usually stamped with the patent date, and are often marked with the inventor's name and address.

The early-19th-century lamps above burned whale oil, while patent lamps, left, made mainly from 1850 to 1870, used lard or camphene.

Laundry Equipment

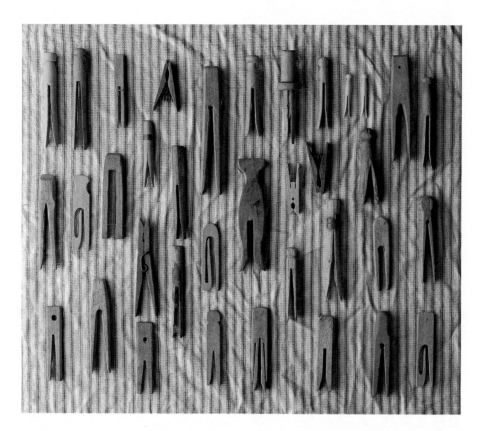

I n the 19th century, an entire day every week was customarily devoted to the heavy work of washing and ironing. The woman of the house began "laundry day" by placing the wash in wooden tubs along with homemade lye or caustic-soda soap. The laundry was agitated with a wooden wash stick or clothes fork; these implements might be finely carved and were often presented as wedding gifts. Particularly dirty clothes were scrubbed on a washboard, which usually had a scrubbing surface made of corrugated wood, tin, cast iron, or glass—or of wooden rollers, spools, or beads. A "wash skate" made with two or three grooved wooden rollers was also good for scrubbing clothes.

After being squeezed through a hand-cranked wringer, the wash was hung out to dry with clothespins. Designed to hold heavy homespun linens on thick hemp clotheslines, early wooden clothespins were sturdy and large—six inches or more in length. Factory-made clothespins, which included the spring-clip and standard push-on type still used today, did not appear until the end of the 19th century.

The pressing was done with heavy flatirons. Two or more heavy irons were heated on the fire; as the one in use cooled, the wooden handle was removed and reattached to the hot one.

Antique laundry equipment has become highly collectible. Above is a sampling of 19th-century clothespins; at right are washtubs, washboards, agitators, wash sticks, and irons.

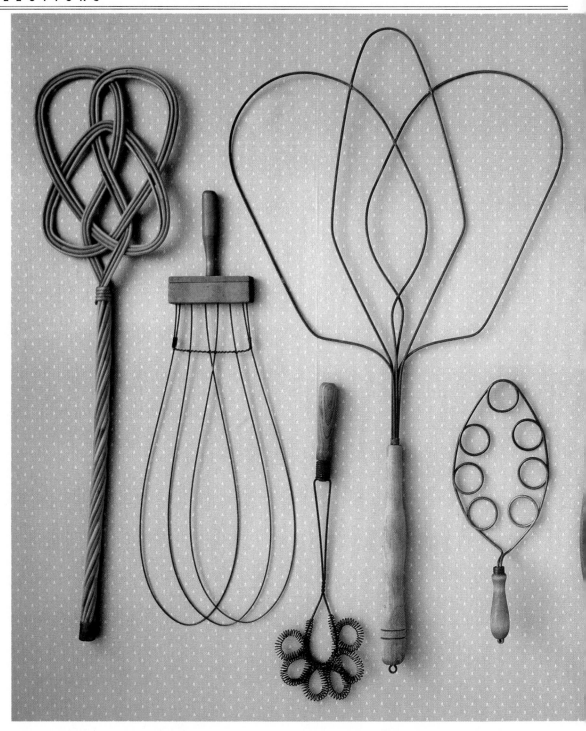

Rug beaters like the 19th- and early-20th-century examples at right were commonly made of wood, rattan, or wire. The twisted rattan beater displays a classic design produced for many decades.

Common in most American households, rug beaters were used from the late 1800s until the early 20th century, when the electric vacuum cleaner began to replace them. These handy tools received especially hard use as part of the annual rite of spring cleaning. It was then that rugs were taken out- side, hung on clotheslines, and given a good beating to remove grime and soot—much of which was produced by the gas and oil lamps of the period.

As many as 150 different types of rug beaters were manufactured in this country. While many were made of wood or rattan, the most common

Rug Beaters

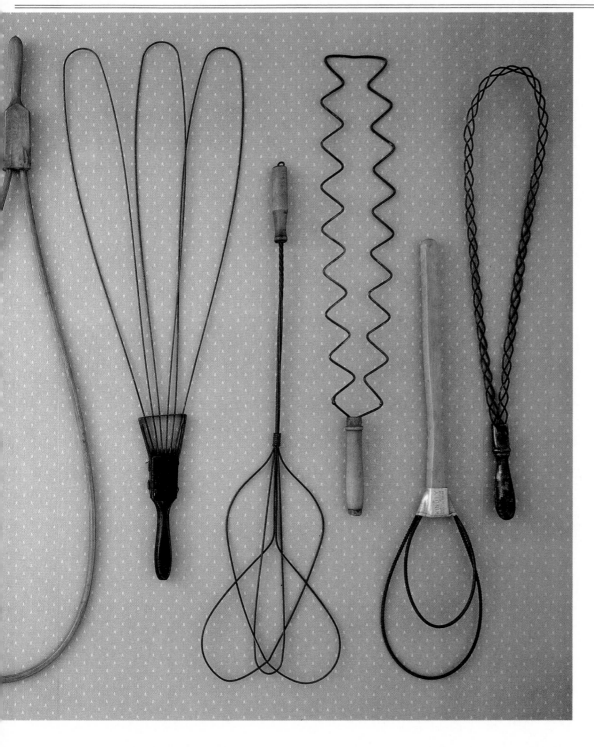

type was fashioned from strands of wire bent into curves, braids, or zigzags. Coiled wire rug beaters are rarer. The basic design of the rug beater did not change considerably over the years, but a few innovations did occur. The introduction of the canted handle in the late 1880s, for example, improved the beater's effi-

ciency while diminishing wear on the knuckles.

Rug beaters are relatively inexpensive and easy to find at antiques fairs and flea markets. Their simple designs often have a striking graphic quality: mounted on a wall, a collection like the one shown above makes a handsome and unusual display.

THE SHAKER WAY

Baskets organized for efficient laundry service

From the late 18th to the early 20th century, the Shakers produced a broad range of goods for the home and the workplace. While these strong-minded pacifists lived in insular, self-contained communities, they were nonetheless enterprising business people and sold many products—including furniture, baskets, brooms, and packaged seeds—to "the world." Outsiders sometimes ridiculed the mystifying religious practices and celibate lifestyle of the Shakers, but they always welcomed Shaker goods for their superior craftsmanship and design.

In addition to products for sale, the Shakers made most of their own household goods and supplies. Industriousness and ingenuity were natural outgrowths of the Shaker way of life; self-sufficiency was not only economical, but also allowed the Shakers independence from their worldly neighbors. Heeding the motto "Hands to work and hearts to God," the Shakers recognized manual labor as a form of worship, and aimed for perfection. "Do all your work as though you had a thousand years to live, and as if you knew you must die tomorrow," admonished

Mother Ann Lee, the founder and spiritual leader of the sect.

·In search of that perfection, the Shakers were dedicated to performing every task they undertook as efficiently as possible. As a result, they invented many laborsaving devices for household cleaning. (According to Mother Ann, dirt was the "devil's doing," and there was none of it in heaven.)

Perhaps the best-known Shaker innovation is the standard flat broom, which can be found in virtually any household today. Until the 1800s, a broom was typically made

Flat brooms, a Shaker invention

by tying a bunch of straw around a handle. The Shakers not only developed a new species of broomcorn—a stiff grass—for the bristles, they also devised a clamp to press the bristles flat so that they could be bound with a straight, broad bottom. These flat brooms could be pushed more easily into corners and under low objects than could the old-fashioned round brooms. By 1805 the Shakers were selling the flat brooms to the public, and they soon developed a thriving cottage industry that included push brooms, whiskbrooms, clothesbrushes, shoebrushes, and even floor mops. The brooms became so popular that for many housekeepers in the early 19th century, a "new broom" meant a Shaker-made broom.

The Shakers devoted special attention to efficiency in their everyday housekeeping. Not only did they invent and patent a type of large-capacity washing machine, but these

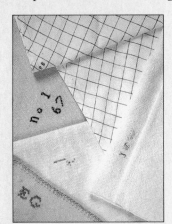
Embroidery-marked linens

enterprising people also created a special stove that could heat twelve flatirons a day, and devised a means for steam-drying laundry indoors. To simplify sorting on laundry days, they marked their household linens and clothing with initials and numbers in extremely plain cross-stitch embroidery. (The Shaker Millennial Laws forbade the use of overly decorative stitchery.) For orderly delivery—laundry services in a single community might extend to more than one hundred people—laundry baskets were numbered and labeled. Several styles of wooden hangers were designed to correspond to the shoulder contouring in men's and women's clothes so that dresses and jackets would hang correctly in the closet. And wooden stocking forms, used for shaping knitted hose as they dried, were individually marked and grouped according to size.

Order and efficiency also extended to the kitchen. Although the Shakers did not manufacture flatware or pottery, they produced nearly everything else that was needed for

cooking. One of their inventions was a cradle-style butter churn—essentially a large box with rockers—that made it possible to produce a sizable amount of butter without the exertion of up-and-down churning. Another Shaker innovation to lighten the work in the kitchen was a grooved rolling pin that was designed to press the last drops of buttermilk out of fresh butter to keep it from becoming rancid.

What the Shakers didn't invent, they improved. The oval-shaped

Wooden stocking forms organized by size

pantry boxes that are usually associated with the sect, for example, were commonly made in America, but it was the Shakers who made them in nests and modified the standard design. Their finely crafted boxes are distinguished by "finger" joints, which would not buckle or shrink with changes in humidity. The joints were secured with copper tacks that could not rust and stain the wood. As with all of the goods made by the sect, the boxes were honest products of the Shaker faith, well-designed for their purpose and excellent in their craftsmanship.

Needlework Accessories

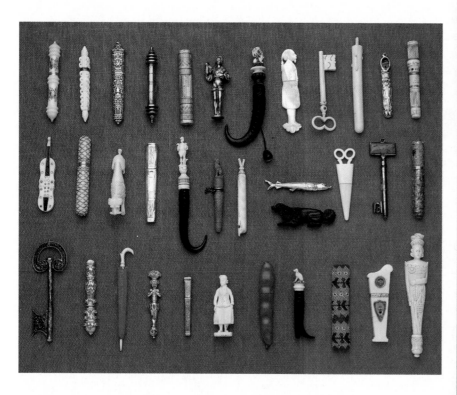

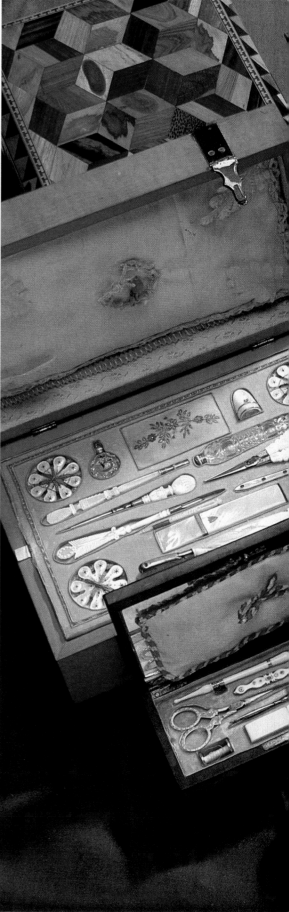

The collection of needlecases above includes prized pieces made from a variety of materials, including precious metals, bone, and even lava. The 18th-century ivory case portraying a fisherwoman is a design made only in Dieppe, France; the 19th-century beadwork case is from Austria.

At one time, a good part of a woman's day was devoted to sewing—whether it be mending clothing and linens or practicing embroidery and other fancywork. The numerous accessories used for such tasks have long held a fascination for collectors, in part because so many are beautifully designed.

Indeed, many of the sewing accessories found today date from the 18th and 19th centuries, when needlecases like those above, and sewing boxes like the ones at right, were conceived more as decorative objects than as strictly utilitarian pieces. Embellished with carving, enamel, and inlay, they were among the few personal items a man could decorously give to a woman.

Continued

The 1850s sewing boxes and étuis at right were imported to America from Europe and England.

Early needlework tools were often as pretty as they were useful. The decorative pincushions above left include a pin-decorated satin example and an 18th-century needlepoint cushion worked in the "queen stitch." The collection of thimbles above right features pieces made of coconut shell, porcelain, gold, silver, and brass, some of which are enameled.

While needlecases were popular in the Victorian era, their use dates back to the 17th century, when needles, handmade from bronze or steel, were rare and always carefully stored. By the 1800s, needles sized for embroidery, quilting, darning, and other types of sewing had become readily available, but the tradition of keeping them in pretty containers continued.

Most of the needlecases found in America were actually made in England and Europe; some were purchased as souvenirs, but many others came with sewing box sets. Because the individual tools in sewing boxes—and in the smaller cases known as *étuis*—have often been removed and sold separately, complete sets are highly prized. If the pieces are original to the box, the tools will fit perfectly in the niches provided for them. Checking the tools for patent marks helps collectors determine the date of an antique set.

Among the other sewing accessories that are especially attractive to collectors are pincushions like the colorful examples above left, which date from the 18th to the early 20th century. Victorian pincushions were often pieced, embroidered, and decorated with beadwork in the fashion of the crazy quilts of the period. Many were also ornamented with designs made with the pins themselves; these were often presented as gifts.

Thimbles like those above right have also become the focus of many sewing collections. They range from utilitarian steel examples produced as 19th-century advertising giveaways to pieces made of porcelain, precious metals,

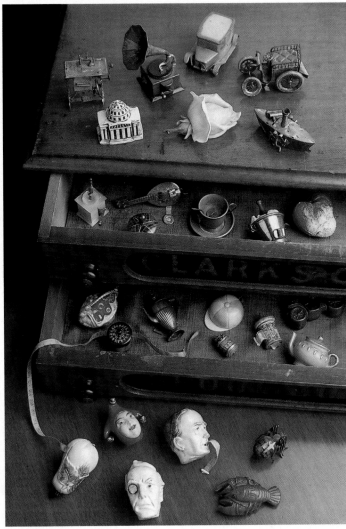

and jewels. Since thimbles—even the elaborate ones—were put to hard use by seamstresses, collectors should examine them for cracks and minute holes, which can diminish their value.

Scissors and scissors cases also were made in a great variety of materials, including gold and ivory. Those above left date from the mid-1600s through the 1800s; among the earliest are a pair of Persian hollow-steel scissors that fold into a dagger shape, and a silver filigree scissors case made in southern Europe. Even plain scissors were frequently stored in elaborate cases that were hung from a ribbon at the waist: today, such cases are usually found without their original scissors. Small Victorian embroidery scissors, made of steel or silver and sometimes trimmed with mother-of-pearl, are relatively

common, but figural pieces such as the hunter and Robinson Crusoe scissors shown here are quite rare.

Equally intriguing are tape measures, above right, that wind into small cases. These have been made since the early 17th century, but most found today date from the mid-19th century or later. Sold as souvenirs or given away as advertising premiums, tape measures typically took the form of small toys. Some were produced in a series, their designs inspired, for example, by well-known buildings or famous politicians. Nineteenth-century tin tape measures frequently incorporate the winder into the design; it might, for example, appear as an automobile crank, or as the handle of a coffee grinder or phonograph.

Sewing scissors like those above left, made from the 1600s to the 1800s, often were crafted in figural shapes; clever designs might incorporate hats or legs, for example, in the handles or blades. Tape measures made in the 19th and early 20th centuries, such as those above right, often took the form of miniature mechanical toys.

Collectible Buttons

Few objects offer more choices to the collector than buttons. Over four hundred types, or "categories," are recognized today; those shown here and on the following two pages are among the limited categories made in America during the 19th and early 20th centuries. Particular favorites are the 19th-century Rockingham-glazed buttons, top right. These were designed to imitate the mottled brown decoration of Rockingham pottery, popular in this country from about 1850 to 1890. While many potteries throughout New England and the Midwest were known for their Rockingham dishware, it is believed that most of the Rockingham buttons came from the Norwalk Potteries, in Norwalk, Connecticut.

Calico buttons, middle right, made of white china and printed with transfer designs, were inspired by the patterns in cotton yard goods. Calico buttons were so well loved that at least three hundred different patterns were printed in America, as well as in England and France, during the second half of the 1800s. Collectors look for those with clear, fresh colors, and for the rare examples that measure an inch or larger.

Buttons made from tintypes—a kind of early photograph printed on iron plate—like those at bottom right, were first made in the 1860s. During the Civil War, it was customary for a soldier to stitch a button bearing the tintype of a

Popular 19th-century American buttons include those with Rockingham glazes (top), calico buttons (middle), and tintype buttons (bottom).

38

loved one to the underside of his lapel. Most tintype buttons are printed with a single portrait; those with two or three are unusual.

Another intriguing button type, the picture button, top left, was popular from the 1800s into the 20th century. Picture buttons were typically made of brass, white metal, or other alloys. Their designs commemorated timely events, like the opening of the Brooklyn Bridge, depicted celebrities, like automobile racer Barney Oldfield, or recorded popular activities of the day. The all-time favorite picture button among collectors is based on a Currier & Ives print, "Skating in Central Park." Equally desirable are large picture buttons—they can be found measuring up to one and one-half inches.

All buttons made after 1900 are known as moderns. The category includes many distinctive types, such as the brass work buttons at middle left. Manufactured during the early part of the century, these buttons were used on overalls and other work clothes. Some are printed with clothing brand names and others with slogans of labor unions. For many collectors, work buttons are interesting for their association with the development of the American labor movement and related industries.

Quite different in feeling are paperweight buttons, like those at bottom left. Beginning in the 1940s, makers of glass paperweights were occa-

Continued

Picture buttons (top), work buttons (middle), and delicate paperweight buttons (bottom) are all prized by collectors.

Moderns, or buttons made in the 20th century, include Bakelite abstracts, above left, and plastic realistics, above right. The plates of food, the vegetable basket, and the cornucopia were hand-painted by Marian Weaver, a famous button designer of the 1930s.

sionally asked to try their hand at miniature versions in buttons made exclusively for collectors. The process was extremely difficult, and very few paperweight buttons were ever made. Charles Kaziun, a famous American paperweight craftsman, reported that he had ruined twenty buttons before he succeeded in producing one with a good design.

As plastic became available beginning in the 1930s, buttons were increasingly produced in this inexpensive, versatile material. In particular, Bakelite, an early type of plastic that could be molded, carved, or inlaid, caught the imagination of button manufacturers. Bakelite buttons like those above left, known as abstracts, made a bolder, more colorful fashion statement than did any of the earlier types.

Also produced from the 1930s to the 1950s were the buttons known as realistics, or goofies, above right. Usually made of plastic (although a

few can be found in wood or glass) they were generally designed as miniature fruits, toys, animals, and household objects. High-quality realistics were not only hand-carved, but also hand-painted. One of the best-known button designers of the period, Marian Weaver, made sets of hand-painted realistics; these might feature a number of different kinds of nuts, an assortment of vegetables, or a half-dozen *plats du jour*. Weaver's designs were considered expensive when they sold for three dollars a set in the 1930s, and they are prized by collectors today.

During the same period, buttons often came sewn onto illustrated cards like those opposite. Many collectors are more interested in the cards (which can occasionally be found at the bottom of an old sewing basket) than in the buttons on them. The most valuable cards are those in good condition with all the buttons intact and with an unusual picture or a photograph of a movie star.

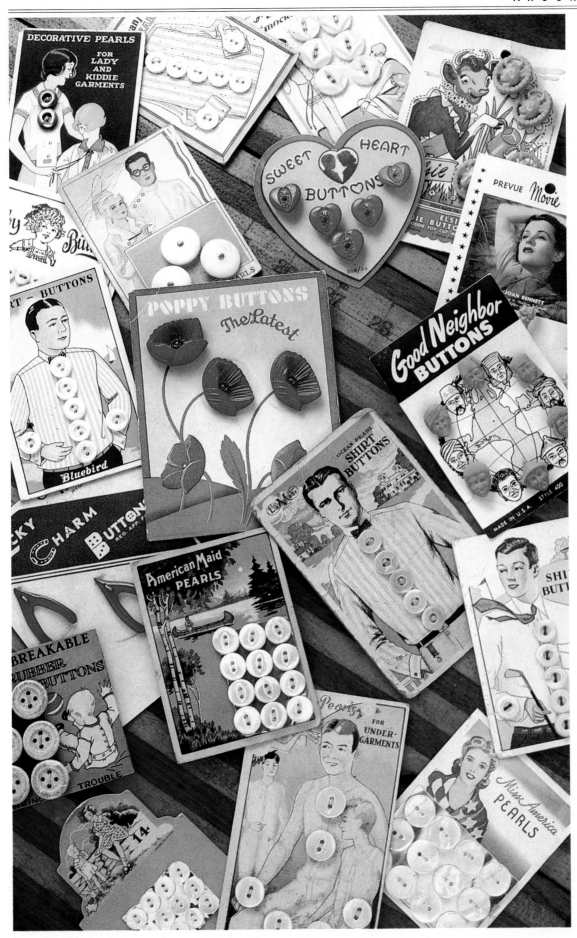

Button cards like those at left, made from the 1930s to the 1950s, often feature provocative images: Elsie the cow, perhaps, or the movie star Joan Bennett. Among the more practical buttons sold on cards were an unbreakable rubber type designed for a child's drop-seat pajamas.

BUTTON COLLAGES

Among the hobby ideas suggested by women's magazines in the 1940s was making collages with buttons. These amusing homemade artworks were simple to craft: color pictures were cut out from magazines or the rotogravure section of the newspaper, glued to a piece of cardboard, then liberally embellished with buttons.

The results depended largely on the collage maker's imagination. Mabel Vickers, a button collector who was in her sixties when she made the button pictures at right, was particularly creative. Along with using cutouts, Vickers often painted in the backgrounds, scenery, and figures herself. She stitched the buttons into colorful borders and sometimes layered the buttons to make three-dimensional floral arrangements. What gives Vickers' pictures their particular charm, however, is the care she took in choosing and matching buttons to her subjects. The little boy in the collage at top right, for example, dangles a fish button from his fishing pole. And many of the figures, including that of Ava Gardner at bottom center, wear jewelry, corsages, or hair ribbons—all carefully composed with buttons.

Button collages, such as those at right made in the 1940s by Mabel Vickers, a button collector, can be found today at flea markets and antiques shops. Appealing for their humor, they can also be a source of rare antique buttons.

Planes and Spokeshaves

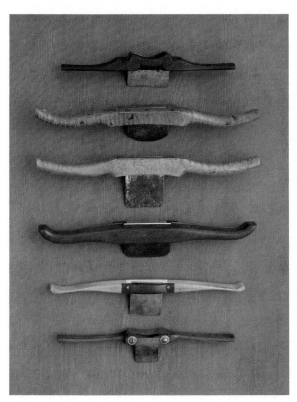

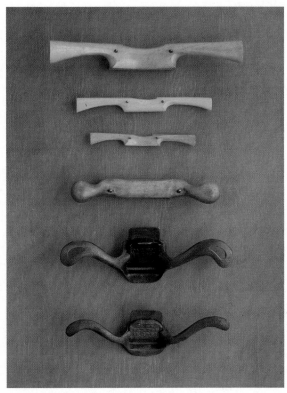

A ntique woodworking tools like the 18th- and 19th-century planes and spokeshaves shown here are intriguing to collectors not only as historical artifacts, but also as objects of fine craftsmanship.

Among the most widely available tools are planes, opposite, which were designed for specific tasks: to smooth wood surfaces, to shape moldings, to carve out grooves, to miter corners, to make the spiraled "spills," or shavings, that served as matches. Signed, handmade 18th-century planes are particularly valuable. The three molding planes at lower right, for example, are signed by Francis Nicholson, John Nich-

olson, and Cesar Chelor, all well-known Massachusetts toolmakers, and are extremely rare. A manufacturer's name and patent date on early iron-and-wood planes, and on the pieces that were made exclusively of iron after the 1870s, increases value. Some collectors specialize by craft, looking for planes used by a shipwright, for example, or a wheelwright.

Handcrafted and factory-made spokeshaves, above left and right, were designed for the precise shaving of surfaces. The tool was typically pushed away from the body as it was used. On some models, the angle of the razor-sharp blade could be adjusted with thumbscrews.

The spokeshaves above left and right were made for precise work: the style of tool that was used depended on the type of wood to be shaved and whether the surface was flat or rounded. The iron spokeshaves were used by shoemakers and glovemakers to smooth their workbenches.

The antique planes opposite include some that were made specifically for mitering, shaving, smoothing, and cutting grooves. Many were also designed for a particular craft, such as wagon making or piano making.

Tools for Measuring

Travelers, like the 19th-century examples above, "traveled" around the rim of a wheel or barrel, while the operator counted rotations to measure the circumference.

The 19th-century tools shown here were designed to help craftsmen calculate the circumference of circles and measure awkward spaces. The iron travelers above were used by wheelwrights and coopers. As the tool was rolled around the rim of a wheel or barrel, the number of rotations was counted. The same number of rotations would then be used to mea-

sure a strip of iron for a "tire" or a barrel hoop

Calipers, opposite top, which consist of hinged legs, are used to determine external and internal measurements: calipers with turned-in tips measure the outside diameter of an object; those with turned-out tips measure the inside diameter. Dividers, opposite bottom, worked like calipers but could also scribe arcs and circles.

The nineteenth-century calipers and dividers opposite measured diameter and thickness.

The calipers shaped like human legs are whimsical variations on a basic design.

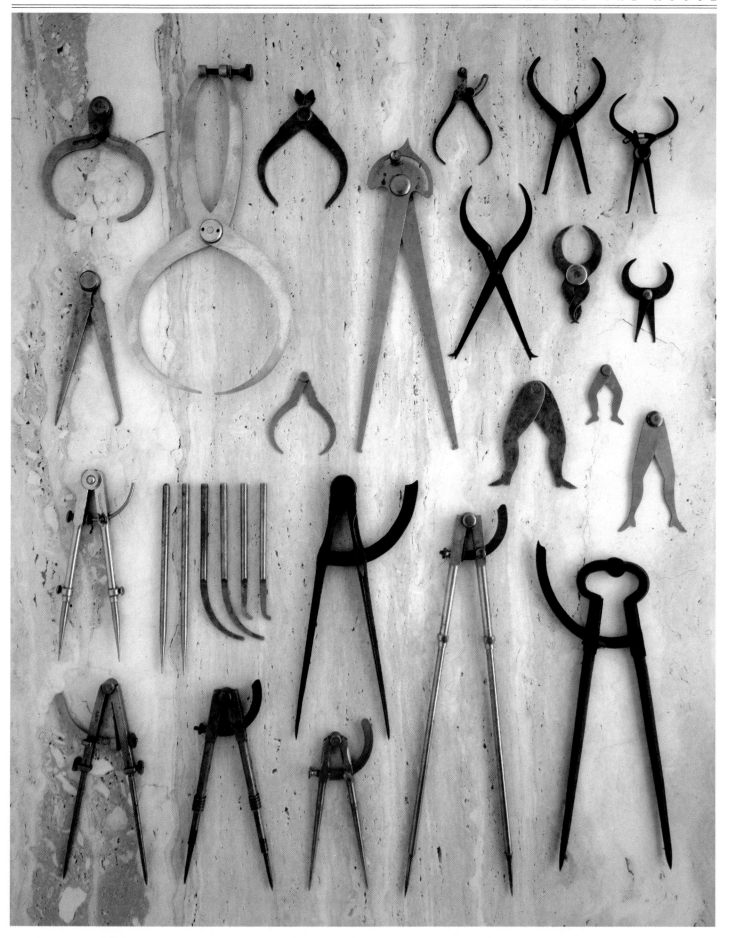

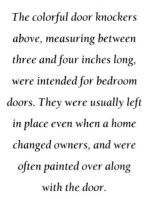

The colorful door knockers above, measuring between three and four inches long, were intended for bedroom doors. They were usually left in place even when a home changed owners, and were often painted over along with the door.

Cast-iron doorstops and door knockers like those pictured here were made primarily from the late 19th century until around 1940. Although both were produced by foundries throughout the Midwest—most firms copied or used each other's molds—the decorative paint finishes were always applied by hand, so no two pieces are exactly alike. The better the paint is preserved, the more desirable the piece. Value is also determined by the rarity of the form. Baskets and vases of flowers, for example, are quite common and account for nearly half of the doorstop and knocker designs produced. More unusual designs depict Queen Victoria, George Washington, and Punch and Judy.

Doorstops and Knockers

The cast-iron doorstops at left were made after the 1860s, when production began in America. The little girl reading a book and the yellow-and-red clown are relatively rare designs.

Butter-making Tools

The churns at right represent a variety of types used in home buttermaking. Large barrel-like cylinder churns could handle as much as five gallons of cream. The small glass churns produced in the late 19th and early 20th centuries could be used on the kitchen table. Another buttermaking collectible is the paddle, used to work the butter after churning.

Prior to the mid-19th century, all butter-making took place at home. It was a laborious process, and from the time the cow was milked until a sweet slab of butter arrived at table or market, many tools were used.

Among the most collectible buttermaking tools are churns. The first butter churns in this country, dating from the mid-17th century, were made like barrels; the butter was worked with a plunger, or dasher. Up-and-down churning required hours of work, but plunger churns—made of white cedar, stoneware, or copper—were nevertheless common until the early 1900s. More innovative models included large barrel-type cylinder churns operated by cranks, and small glass tabletop churns.

Once churned, butter was packed into wooden tubs or molds. The molds were frequently decorated with chip-carved designs that served as the maker's trademark when butter was sold at market. Carved butter prints—usually circular, semicircular, or rectangular in form—were also used to decorate and put a trademark on slabs of butter sold at market; smaller prints marked designs into pats of butter for the table.

The first butter prints and molds were entirely hand-carved. Later prints were turned on lathes and their designs carved by hand; and by the 1860s many prints and molds were being mass-produced. Hand-carved examples are the most desirable; among the rarest are those with animal, bird, and fish designs.

The 19th-century buttermaking tools above include a four-part hinged print for a five-pound butter slab,

a mold that shapes butter into the form of a house, and a scoop with a handle that doubles as a print.

HOME BUTTERMAKING

Dash Churns.

Standard
Barrel Churns.

A NEW DOMESTIC MOTOR.

Before commercial creameries became well established in the mid-19th century, virtually anyone who owned a cow made butter for his own table. It was also common for farm families to make extra money by selling their butter at market.

In general, buttermaking was considered woman's work and was regarded as drudgery. After the cows were milked, the warm milk had to be lugged in buckets from the barn to the house, where it was strained into flat-bottomed earthenware bowls or low wooden tubs—known as keelers—to cool. Once the cream had risen, it was skimmed off the top, and when enough was collected it was placed in a churn. Then the real work began.

Depending on the temperature and the type of churn that was used, it could take as many as three or four hours of cranking or plunging before the butter was formed. The labor-intensive plunger churn with broom-stick handle, which remained standard until the early 1900s, was the most common type used; hand-cranked and mechanically operated churns designed to make the job easier were developed in the 18th and 19th centuries, but they never became as widespread.

When the cream finally "came," it formed tiny granules of butter. Cold

Oval Churns.

water was sometimes added at that point to help the butter granules cohere into one large solid lump. Once the butter was solidified, it was removed from the churn with a wooden scoop, and the remaining liquid—the buttermilk—set aside for cooking or drinking. The butter was then rinsed in cold water, and worked with a grooved rolling pin or a pair of wooden "hands," or paddles, to remove the last traces of but-

termilk, which could sour. Salt was mixed in to help the butter keep, and carrot juice was sometimes added to turn the finished product a healthy yellow color.

The fresh butter was then pressed into molds, or was weighed in pound and half-pound units that would be shaped into mounds with paddles. If a woman owned a butter print, she could then decorate the butter with her mark.

Although men might sometimes milk the cows or take the butter to market, the task of buttermaking nearly always fell to women. As these pictures reveal, churning was accomplished with a variety of devices: one inventive housewife is shown powering her churn—and a cradle—by means of a rocking chair.

Laborsaving Gadgets

The eggbeaters at right were produced by American manufacturers between 1873 and 1940. Brand names like Super Whirl, Lightning, Big Bingo, Whippo, Cyclone, and Jiffywhip advertised the timesaving virtues of such gadgets.

Even the earliest kitchen utensils were laborsaving devices, but it was not until the Industrial Revolution that innovative mechanical gadgets began to appear on the American market. Among the most welcome were apple parers and eggbeaters.

Throughout the 18th and 19th centuries, apples were a mainstay of the American diet: each fall, an ample supply was pared, sliced, and dried for winter use. The first patented parer, made of wood and metal, appeared around 1803. But it was not until mid-century that cast-iron parers with spring-activated steel blades became available. On all models the apple turned while the blade followed the fruit's contour.

By 1874, over eighty patents had been granted for apple parers (some of these gadgets cored and segmented apples as well) and the numbers increased as the century progressed. Most parers are marked with their patent date and number.

Patents were also taken out for eggbeaters—as early as 1856—but the first mass-produced model did not appear until 1870, a product of the Dover Stamping Company. The original Dover beater and later models were so successful that, until around 1900, any eggbeater was called a Dover no matter who the manufacturer actually was. Between the 1870s and 1930s, Dover and other companies offered dozens of types, each one "new and improved."

Most early eggbeaters have cast-iron rotary gears; a beater made with steel gears probably dates from the turn of the century or later. The company name and the patent date are generally stamped on the gear. A variation on the hand-held beaters was a type that came with a splash-guard, or apron, that fit on top of a special jar, crock, or pitcher.

The utensils for preparing apples above, made between 1860 and 1890, include cast-iron

parers and tools used for segmenting the fruit.

Grinders and Graters

The wooden mortars and pestles above were made over a time span of several hundred years. Although a mortar was typically crafted of the same material as the accompanying pestle, the two parts in the antique sets found today may not necessarily match.

Mortars and pestles have been used since ancient times by apothecaries and tobacconists as well as by cooks. Both the mortar (the bowl section) and the pestle (the grinder) were traditionally made of the same material. This might be a hardwood, stone, glass, or porcelain, or any hard substance that does not absorb odors. The woods in American-made mortars and pestles crafted from the 1600s onward are typically burled maple and ash, as well as bird's-eye maple. The woods more commonly used for English and European pieces include olive, lignum vitae, and oak.

Like mortars and pestles, nutmeg graters of both American and English make can be found in great variety. (Nutmeg, a hard, aromatic seed native to the East Indies, was used as a food seasoning in America as early as the 1600s.) Most graters are formed from pierced tin—usually curved to protect the fingers during grating—and are sometimes made with a small box at one end for storing the ungrated nutmegs. Mechanical nutmeg graters with crank handles or with spring mechanisms designed to hold the nutmeg against the grater were made during the second half of the 19th century. Many mechanical graters were patented and these usually bear a patent date.

The nutmeg graters opposite date from the 17th to the late 19th century. The egg-shaped silver and ivory graters are a pocket type once carried by travelers. The tin shoe grater may be one of a kind.

The tin cookie cutters at right were made during the first half of the 19th century. "Sugar-cookie" cutters, which produce a wavy star shape, are not hard to find today. The most sought-after shapes include birds, hearts, hands, and animals, especially horses.

Tin Cutters

Tin cookie and biscuit cutters have been used in America since the 1700s. As in the European tradition, whimsically shaped cutters were favored for cookies, while simple round cutters were generally used for biscuits; both types of cutters are collected today.

Early cookie cutters were handcrafted by tinsmiths who sold them along with pots, pans, and other household wares. The shape of the cutter—perhaps a human figure, heart, or animal—was formed from an inch-wide strip of tin that was seamed with a soldered joint and then soldered to a tin backing; often a handle was added. When manufacturers began mass-producing cookie cutters in the mid-1800s, they simply copied the earlier designs. Manufactured cutters typically have more uniform shapes and soldering than handmade versions.

Early biscuit cutters were also made of tin until the 1930s, when manufacturers started producing both types of cutters in aluminum. Many of the biscuit cutters that date from the late 1800s and early 1900s were given away as premiums by flour and kitchen-range companies.

The biscuit cutters above date from the 1850s to the 1920s. The round cutters in the foreground were made as advertising giveaways.

Chocolate and Ice Cream Molds

Hinged pewter ice cream molds like those above were produced by both American and European manufacturers. Teddy bears were a favorite subject in the 1920s; motorcycles became popular a decade later.

From the mid-1800s through the first half of the 20th century, chocolate and ice cream companies used metal molds to shape their confections. The subjects of the mold designs changed through the years as hundreds of different patterns were produced by manufacturers in America, France, and Germany.

The molds made between 1880 and 1910 are considered the classics: the realistic shapes, including animals such as rabbits and cows, were finely modeled and detailed. Between 1910 and 1930, the molds took on a streamlined look in keeping with Art Deco design, and fanciful subjects such as teddy bears, doll-like children, and rabbits dressed like people became popular. Molds made between 1930 and 1950, in turn, reflect a widespread interest in Walt Disney characters as well as a fascination with cars, planes, and motorcycles.

While the subjects for ice cream and chocolate molds were similar, the materials were different. Ice cream molds were usually made of pewter. Various tin-plated nickel alloys were used to produce chocolate molds, since pewter was too soft and porous for use with molten chocolate. These chocolate molds sometimes doubled as molds for ice cream.

Like ice cream molds, many chocolate molds consisted of two halves that, when hinged or clamped together, produced three-dimensional figures. There were also "flats" for making chocolates with a one-sided design.

Made in the late 1800s and early 1900s, the chocolate molds at left include "flats" and three-dimensional forms. Molds from the turn of the century are usually more finely modeled and detailed than those made in subsequent decades.

Country Redware

R edware, a type of red or reddish-brown earthenware, was the first pottery made in America. Although widely produced throughout the 18th and 19th centuries, examples dating from before 1800 are scarce because this porous, brittle pottery breaks easily.

One early and common technique for decorating redware was "sliptrailing," in which thinned clay, colored black or yellow, was applied in flourishes or used to write out words. The range of colors was limited in the 1700s because the metallic oxides used for glazes had to be im-

Like most redware found today, these pieces date from the 19th century. With the exception of the yellow cup, which is English, they were all made in this country. The pieces with green glazes are rare: copper oxide, which produces the color, was expensive and difficult for potters to obtain.

ported from Europe, at great cost, or dug and ground by hand. By the mid-1800s, however, glazing materials had become more readily available and the decoration—including bright solid-color glazes and those that were dotted and streaked with brown—more varied.

Eventually it was discovered that the clear lead-base glaze that was used to seal the clay on redware pieces was poisonous. While this fact was published as early as 1785 and widely known by the 1830s, the pottery was still produced with the glaze until late in the 1800s.

Decorative Jaspé

Made for everyday use in French country kitchens and restaurants, jaspé—a type of decorated redware—was produced primarily from the 18th century until the 1930s. Considerably less expensive than American redware, it has only recently appeared on the American antiques market, and is becoming increasingly popular among collectors.

Jaspé is the product of French potters in towns along the Swiss and German borders of the Alsace region, where iron-rich clay is found in abundance. The French word, which means

Traditional decoration on jaspé pottery pieces such as those at left includes marbleized patterns, polka dots, and bands of intersecting diamonds. The most common forms are pitchers, mugs, and tureens.

mottled or variegated, refers to the colorful glazes that distinguish many pieces. Other typical jaspé decoration includes polka dots and simple birds, flowers, houses, and hearts. These designs are usually drawn as outlines, then filled in with colors that include a variety of bright primary shades as well as black, cream, and green.

Among the most common forms of jaspé are pitchers, mugs, and tureens. Rarer pieces include large platters, sconces, and wall boxes. Most jaspé found today dates from the late 19th and early 20th centuries.

Salt-Glazed Stoneware

Salt-glazed stoneware imported from Germany and England was used in America from the time of the earliest settlements. A few American potteries began producing a small amount of stoneware by the early 18th century, but production did not become widespread until a century later.

Made from clay that can be fired at high temperatures in a kiln, stoneware pottery is extremely durable, as is the clear salt glaze used to seal the clay. While the pottery is being fired, salt is tossed into the kiln; the salt vaporizes and settles on the clay in transparent drops. As the pottery cools, the clay surface takes on a light gray or buff color and the texture of an orange peel.

Throughout the 19th century, American-produced stoneware satisfied the demand for a durable utilitarian pottery: it was never made as tableware but rather as simple jugs, jars, crocks, and even butter churns for the pantry and kitchen. Sometimes left plain, the pottery was more typically decorated—like earlier German stoneware—with incised drawings detailed in cobalt-blue glaze; designs were also brushed on in blue.

By 1860, all the finer pieces of stoneware on the market were decorated with pictorial designs in blue. Collectors are particularly interested in those decorated with animals, human figures, and sailing ships; simple floral motifs and flourishes are more common. Many potteries stamped their wares with their name and location; for collectors with regional interests, such a mark can enhance the value of a piece.

Although salt-glazed stoneware like the 19th-century American pieces at left was made as utilitarian pottery, it was nevertheless frequently decorated. Unusual designs, such as the spotted horse and deer, and the unflattering portrait of Billy McGue, add to the value of a piece.

Rockingham Pottery

Between 1835 and 1890 virtually every sizable pottery in America produced Rockingham pieces like those at right. Patterns were copied from English pottery companies and were reproduced widely, which makes it difficult to determine the origin of an object. Pieces were individually spattered with brown glaze; consequently no two are alike.

Rockingham pottery takes its name from the Marquis of Rockingham, whose 19th-century potteryworks in Swinton, England, turned out wares with a mottled brown glaze that resembled tortoiseshell.

Beginning in the mid-1800s, the Lyman, Fenton & Co. pottery in Vermont was among the first to make Rockingham in America; soon nearly one hundred other potteries located in Pennsylvania, Ohio, New Jersey, New York, Maryland, and Vermont followed suit. Their inexpensive brown-decorated wares, generally cast from molds, ranged from simple mugs and baking pans to specialized pieces such as picture frames, flasks, foot warmers, doorknobs, and cuspidors.

American potters copied not only the glaze used on English Rockingham but also the shapes and designs. Among the forms favored by collectors are Toby jugs, cow-shaped creamers, hound-handled pitchers, and pitchers made with raised panels or with biblical scenes such as "Rebekah at the Well."

The use of molds meant that Rockingham pottery could be made in a wide variety of forms. Above, the large Toby jug depicts "Rough and Ready" Zachary Taylor, the smaller pitcher shows a landscape scene, and the cuspidor is decorated with molded scallop shells.

THE POTTERIES OF BENNINGTON

To some pottery collectors, "Bennington" signifies salt-glazed stoneware. To others, the name indicates pottery with a mottled brown glaze. There were, in fact, more than a dozen kinds of pottery and porcelain produced in the two potteries that existed in Bennington, Vermont, during the 1800s.

The first Bennington pottery, the Norton Company, was established by Captain John Norton in 1793 and remained in operation as a family business for 101 years. Norton began production with redware, but soon changed to stoneware, which was to become the company's specialty.

In 1845, Julius Norton, a grandson of the founder, brought his brother-in-law Christopher Fenton in as a partner but the collaboration lasted only two years. Fenton wanted to add English-style pottery to the line, but while he was able to convince the Norton Company to produce Rockingham pottery and some simple yellow-glazed wares, stoneware remained the primary product of the company.

Full of ideas, Fenton opened his own company in Bennington in 1847. It was known first as Lyman, Fenton & Co., and later as the United States Pottery Company. The business failed and by 1858 was closed. During those eleven years, however, Fenton produced a broad array of ceramics including Rockingham and an unglazed white porcelain called Parian. Fenton also devised a glazing method called flint enamel that produced a glowing brown finish shot through with color. By employing English designers, Fenton achieved the look he was after, and his "fancy wares" became an important influence on other 19th-century American ceramics manufacturers.

Among these pieces from the two 19th-century potteries that were located in Bennington, Vermont, are a book-shaped flask, an ornamental poodle, and a hound-handled pitcher—all Rockingham— and a flint enamel ribbed slop jar with top.

Colorful Spongeware

Spongeware—any pottery whose decoration has been dabbed or sponged on for a mottled effect—was introduced from England to America sometime after 1830. While it was a utilitarian ware, its cheerful glazing patterns were intended to make life in the kitchen a bit brighter.

Spongeware pieces used for storage, food preparation, and simple table settings were, in fact, a staple in American kitchens and pantries. Because this versatile pottery was ovenproof, spongeware stewpots, casseroles, and baking pans were also common. Although some early pieces were made with white clay, most spongeware was crafted of stoneware or yellowware clay, which rendered it extremely durable.

Manufactured at large potteries throughout New Jersey and the Midwest, spongeware was inexpensive to produce. As an incentive for housewives to buy, many food companies sold products such as butter and mustard in spongeware crocks and jugs marked with their logo and an advertising slogan.

Because spongeware was produced in abundance until the 1940s, it can still be easily found. Most pieces on the market date from the turn of the century and later. Many sponging patterns and colors were used during that period: blue and white was a popular combination and remains so today. Pieces sponged with two colors over a third are among the most valuable. Teapots, large platters, stewpots with hinged wire handles, trivets, and tall-sided soda-fountain mugs are the rarest forms.

The spongeware pieces at left are typical examples of this durable kitchenware, made from the late 1800s to the 1940s. Although single bowls are plentiful, sets of nesting bowls such as those on the bottom shelf are difficult to find, and sets of more than four are extremely rare.

Enameled
Graniteware

I n the mid-1800s, American manufacturers began to experiment with coating iron cookware with glasslike glazes to protect against rust. By the 1870s enameled ironware was on the market. As American steel production increased late in the century, enamel was applied to steel as well. Produced by dozens of companies throughout the Midwest and Middle Atlantic states, enameled kitchenwares were sold under many different names but are now collectively known as graniteware.

Graniteware made from steel was especially

appealing to the Victorian housewife because it was far lighter than the cast-iron cookware to which she was accustomed. The enameled surface made it easy to clean, and a broad selection of designs and patterns, which included speckles, swirls, and florals, were available in numerous colors. Some pieces, such as coffeepots and sugar bowls made for use at the table, were trimmed with white handles and lids. These, as well as miniature tea sets, match safes, and salt boxes, are among the rarer graniteware items sought by collectors today.

Graniteware—enameled metalware—was immensely popular from 1870 to 1930, when aluminum cookware was introduced. Pieces like those at left were also known as glazed-ware, agateware, and speckleware. The origin of the term graniteware is uncertain, but it may derive from the colorful patterns of the enamel, which can resemble the variegated patterns in the stone.

Setting the Table

*pewter, china, glassware,
and linens prized by collectors*

On the following pages, you will find a broad selection of wares that have had a familiar place on American dining tables from colonial times until well into the 20th century. Some, like pewter, were crafted by hand. But the vast majority of tablewares available today are products of the Industrial Revolution. Mass-produced glass and transfer-printed china, for example, had become widely available by the late 1800s. While such pieces are traditional favorites among collectors, the inexpensive tablewares introduced in the Depression era, such as Fiestaware and Harlequinware, are also becoming increasingly popular.

Because they were generally produced in quantity, and therefore can be fairly easily found, tablewares like those on the following pages offer an irresistible invitation to the collector. Pressed glass and Staffordshire, for example, are frequently seen at antiques fairs and flea markets; collectors enjoy the challenge of assembling a complete set of tableware in the same pattern. Buying a single piece at first—a salt cellar, perhaps, or a platter— can be the beginning of a lifetime of collecting.

Antique dinner plates include examples of Gaudy Dutch, Flow Blue, and transfer ware.

PEWTER MARKS

This banner was carried by the New York Society of Pewterers in a 1788 parade celebrating ratification of the United States Constitution.

The touch marks, or "touches," that are stamped into many antique pewter pieces originally served two functions: they identified the maker by name and location, and indicated the quality of metal that was used. In England and Europe, pewterers were required to use these marks under the strict laws enforced by craftsmen's guilds from medieval times.

In America, the first pewterers were immigrant craftsmen who had learned their trade as apprentices in England. But while they formed professional societies, the guild tradition did not take hold in this country, and American pewterers were never re-

quired to mark their wares. In spite of this, most of them did, perhaps through habit, and perhaps as a means of advertising.

American touch-mark designs changed as the country developed. The earliest ones typically incorporated a maker's initials, but by the 1700s full names had also begun to appear on pewter plates and porringers. Prior to the Revolutionary War, many pewterers used English-style pictorial marks: a ship, a lion, or the royal symbol of the rose and crown might be depicted.

After 1776, pewterers began featuring the American eagle, adapting symbols from their state seals, or

making logos from their own names.

After 1825, pewterers had to step up production to compete with the increasing availability of silverplate and porcelain tablewares. Touch marks gradually lost their individualized look and were reduced to business names and addresses.

Shown opposite are a few of the hundreds of American pewter marks known today. (The dates represent the period when the mark was used.) When attempting to identify a mark, you should use extreme care: more than one pewterer used the same initials; others employed more than one mark; and some touch marks are forgeries.

David Melville
Newport, Rhode Island
c. 1776-1793

William Bradford, Jr.
New York City
c. 1719-1758

Brook Farm
West Roxbury, Massachusetts
c. 1844-1847

Nathaniel Austin
Charlestown, Massachusetts
c. 1763-1807

Hiram Yale
Wallingford, Connecticut
c. 1822-1831

Ebenezer Southmayd
Castleton, Vermont
c. 1802-1820

Robert Palethorp, Jr.
Philadelphia
c. 1817-1822

Frederick Bassett
New York City; Hartford, Connecticut
c. 1761-1799

John Bassett
New York City
c. 1720-1761

William Elsworth
New York City
c. 1767-1798

Thomas D. and Sherman Boardman
Hartford, Connecticut
c. 1810-1850

Thomas Danforth III
Philadelphia; Stepney, Connecticut
c. 1777-1819

Historical Ware

Sometimes known as "Old Blue," blue historical Staffordshire pieces like those at right and above display a few of the many patterns that were designed for the American market. A favorite subject was General Lafayette's 1824 visit to America. A rare and very valuable design is the "States" border pattern, in which a ribbon of the names of the states of the Union is used to decorate the rim of a piece.

Staffordshire pottery is named for the English county where much of the pottery exported to this country in the 1800s was made. Produced until about 1860 specifically for the American market, pictorial pieces like those shown here are known as historical ware. Their colorful transfer-printed patterns, which portrayed famous statesmen, commemorated historical events, and celebrated American technological advances, were designed to appeal to the patriotic spirit of a proud new nation.

Historical ware was a relatively inexpensive, everyday dinnerware that was sold widely across this country. The transfer patterns were made possible by a timesaving process introduced in the 1750s that involved copperplate printing; this method also made them far cheaper to produce than hand-painted designs. The dark blue used for printing early Staffordshire was the most popular color and remains so today. Historical ware is also available in the light blue, green, sepia, pink, and mulberry colors that technological advances made possible after the 1830s. The subject, the rarity of the design, and the sharpness of the pattern affect the value of a piece.

Light-colored historical Staffordshire dinnerware, such as the pieces above, was made after 1830, when a higher grade of pottery came into use. Potters decorated the Staffordshire in single colors as well as combinations.

Displayed at right is a collection of lusterware, an English pottery that is characterized by a metallic sheen. Commemorative pieces like the two pitchers on the bottom shelf that feature portraits of Andrew Jackson and Benjamin Harrison are highly valued. The pink pieces are a type of "splash" lusterware known as Sunderland, which is distinguished by a mottled decoration.

Antique Lusterware

L usterware, an English pottery imported to America primarily during the first half of the 19th century, was designed to imitate silver and other metal wares. Characterized by an iridescent sheen, the decorative pieces were coated with a thin film—colored silver, copper, gold, pink, or purple—that was produced when a metallic solution was fused to the ceramics after they were glazed. Platinum, first available in the 1790s, yielded silver; the other colors were made with gold.

Produced by about fifty potteries, lusterware was used for tea and dessert services as well as for bowls, pitchers, and jugs. The early pieces were lustered inside and out in solid colors. By about 1830, solid-color bands and flower motifs had been introduced as decoration, and pieces were being made with white linings. As the decoration became more varied, the metallic luster was combined with hand-painted or relief designs. Many pieces were also treated with a "resist" technique, in which a design was applied with a material, like wax, that resisted the metallic solution. After a piece was lustered, the "resist" was removed, leaving a contrasting pattern.

A rare and desirable type of lusterware is called canary luster. This pottery is decorated with bright yellow glazes and transfer designs, including mottoes and rhymes. Another type of lusterware, with a pink or lilac "splash" finish, is Sunderland, named for the region in England where most of it was produced.

The collection above includes examples of bright yellow canary luster; silver lusterware, designed to imitate tableware made of real silver; and "resist"-decorated pieces.

THE CHINA TRADE

Domestically made wares always had a place on American tables, but even as early as the 1600s there was a strong demand for foreign goods in the colonies. After America had won its independence and was freed from the restrictive trade policies of England, the young nation was particularly eager to enter the arena of world commerce. The vast Chinese empire—whose resources had been tapped by Europeans since the 1500s—attracted any enterprising seaman willing to risk the perilous voyage to the East in return for wealth and adventure.

While the self-sufficient Chinese neither wanted nor needed to trade with the West, Americans coveted such Oriental luxuries as silk, tea, and porcelain. To tempt Chinese merchants, American traders offered them silver coins, tobacco, furs, and ginseng, as well as spices they had acquired en route in the East Indies. The *Empress of China*, the first American ship to enter the port of Canton, arrived in 1784; by 1800, business was so successful that some thirty ships were setting sail for China annually from American ports.

As international commerce developed between the late 18th and mid-19th centuries, Chinese workshops produced art works, textiles, and furnishings intended specifically for the American market. Among the most popular products was the porcelain now known as Chinese export and often erroneously called Lowestoft. (It was once thought that Chinese-style ceramics were made at a pottery in Lowestoft, England.)

Chinese export porcelain was produced primarily at Ch'ing-te Chen, an inland porcelain center, and then shipped to the Cantonese *hongs*, or warehouses, for sale. Many of the wares exported to America were made in stock patterns, including floral, nautical, patriotic, and emblematic designs in bright colors. A favorite motif was the eagle; its sparrowlike appearance, however, reflects the characteristically naive Oriental interpretation of many American subjects. Other stock patterns made for export include three blue-and-white designs—Canton, Nanking, and Fitzhugh—and three ornate patterns in the rose palette: Rose Medallion, Rose Canton, and Mandarin.

Custom-designed pieces, however, were also available. While Europeans ordered dinnerwares emblazoned with coats of arms, Americans usually commissioned wares decorated with monograms, mottoes, or insignia. The porcelain was made primarily in tea sets and in dinner services of many as 350 pieces. Also popular were decorative wares, including the vases and urns that were part of a mantel set.

Goods imported as part of the China trade during the 18th and 19th centuries include, at left, a variety of porcelains, an inlaid tea caddy, and a watercolor painting.

Victorian Majolica

A brightly glazed pottery that appealed to the Victorian taste for color and ornament, majolica was made from the mid- to the late 19th century in both Europe and America.

The name derives from *maiolica*, a tin-glazed earthenware made in Italy between the 1400s and 1600s. Victorian majolica, however, was adapted from the designs of a 16th-century French potter, Bernard Palissy, whose work was characterized by vividly colored lead glazes and naturalistic shapes. The English firm of Minton was the first to revive Palissy's technique: in 1851, its new line of gaudy, inexpensive wares was introduced to great acclaim at the Crystal Palace Exhibition in London. The pottery was soon copied by many English makers, but several American companies also produced the colorful wares. The most noted American firm was Griffin, Smith & Hill, in Pennsylvania, whose very popular Etruscan Majolica line was offered from 1881 until 1892, when the factory burned.

Both English and American majolica are distinguished by lustrous glazes and organically inspired designs rendered in rich relief. Tableware not only was decorated with natural motifs, such as fruits, flowers, and shells, but also often took on their shapes. Pitchers, mugs, cups, and plates, for example, might be modeled and decorated to resemble an ear of corn, a head of cauliflower, or perhaps a bird, a piece of fruit, or a leaf. Pieces in which the form and decoration are wittily combined are among the most highly valued: an oyster plate, for instance, covered with seaweed, a sardine box with a fish-shaped handle, or a basket "woven" to resemble wickerwork. While there is a profusion of majolica tableware, bowls and urns are rare.

The American-made majolica pieces above, called Etruscan Majolica, display some popular motifs such as the shell and the cauliflower. The pieces at right are from European and American potteries.

Toby and Face Jugs

Used for drinking and serving ale, the English and American Toby and face jugs, right, date from the 1830s to 1900. Early Toby jugs are hand-modeled, heavy, and are seldom marked by the maker. Tobies made after the early 1800s were generally mass-produced from molds and were made with lighter clay.

Toby jugs, shaped like human figures, and face jugs, shaped like faces, are ceramic vessels made to hold ale. While face jugs have been known since medieval times, Toby jugs were first made in England in the 1760s. They often portray a portly fellow in 18th-century dress holding a tankard; the crown of his tricorn hat can be removed and used as a cup. The inspiration is thought to be either Sir Toby Belch in *Twelfth Night,* Uncle Toby in *Tristram Shandy*, or Toby Philpot (also spelled Fillpot), hero of a 1761 song,

"The Brown Jug"—prodigious ale-drinkers all.

The first Tobies were made by a Staffordshire potter named Ralph Wood. Wood's pieces stand about ten inches high—tall enough to hold a quart of ale—and are finely detailed in realistic colors. Numerous English and American firms produced variations on the design. In addition to Toby jugs, collectors seek sailors, farmers, and historical, military, and literary characters. Among the few female versions are a milkmaid, a gin drinker, and the Martha Gunn jug, named for a once-famous attendant at Brighton Beach.

DRINKING IN COLONIAL AMERICA

America in colonial times was a nation of drinkers. Alcohol, however, was more a necessity than a social nicety. Early European settlers were unaccustomed to drinking water, which was polluted in most areas of 17th-century Europe, and liquor was considered far safer and more potable. Moreover, a good stiff drink helped ward off the cold, and made hard work a bit more bearable.

Indeed, alcohol was a way of life, and those who abstained were considered "crank-brained." Liquor was ever-present in the home, where children as well as adults imbibed; was doled out regularly to field hands; and was served up at barn-raisings. It also flowed at weddings, funerals, baptisms, public celebrations, militia musters, polling places, and of course, in taverns, which were among the first buildings erected in the colonies.

The favorite colonial drinks were ale and beer, which were dietary staples. When the hops and malt traditionally used to brew these spirits were unavailable, corn, bran, sassafras root, or birch or spruce bark were used instead. The ingenuity of the colonial brewer was celebrated in this verse from the 1630s:

If barley be wanting to make into malt,
We must be content and think it no fault,
For we can make liquor to sweeten our lips,
Of pumpkins, and parsnips, and walnut-tree chips.

A more palatable alternative to such dubious concoctions was rum, the first hard liquor to win favor in the colonies. New Englanders began producing rum from West Indian molasses around 1700. But because transporting the molasses inland was costly, whiskey, distilled from such grains as corn, barley, and rye, became an alternative in frontier areas.

A less potent spirit was apple cider, which was pressed and fermented at home and might accompany any meal. Other fruit drinks were perry, from pears, and peachy, from peaches, as well as wines.

Decorated Earthenware

Two particularly decorative types of pottery that were produced in England for export to America are mochaware and spatterware. Mochaware, made mainly between the 1780s and 1850s, was named for mocha stone—a form of agate found near the Arabian port of Mocha—because the "veins" that decorate many of the pieces resemble the stone's markings. Pieces that feature colored banding are also called banded creamware. Other designs include the squiggly earthworm—or rope twist—pattern and the spotted "cat's eye."

Spatterware, characterized by sponged or spotted decoration, was particularly popular from 1820 to 1860. While spatterware resembles spongeware, the patterns are finer and more precise. In some cases, they are combined with hand-painted or transfer-print designs; in others, bits of sponge, cut into the shapes of leaves, hearts, and roses, were used to create motifs.

The English spatterware displayed above is available in many gaudy colors and patterns, which English potters believed would appeal to the American market. These examples date from the 1820s to the 1850s.

The mochaware pieces opposite date from the 1780s to the 1840s. Made in England, the colorful tableware typically took the form of pitchers, teapots, and mugs; plates are rare.

Children's Tableware

C hildren's tableware, including cups and plates, and tea and dinner services, was made in Europe as early as the 16th century. Originally, these wares were simply smaller versions of those used by adults and were found only in wealthy households. It was not until the Victorian era that mass-produced dishware for small diners became widely available. By this time, children were treated like children—rather than little grown-ups—and the bright colors and lively patterns of the small 19th-century wares were designed specifically to appeal to the young.

Produced primarily in England, children's wares were generally made of pottery such as majolica, stoneware, creamware, lusterware,

and ironstone. Most pieces were decorated with transfer patterns or hand-painted designs—typically flowers, fruits, animals, or landscapes.

Particularly popular among collectors are the plates designed to educate children at mealtimes. The center of the plate features a pictorial design that might be inspired by a biblical story, popular game or sport, historical event, nursery rhyme, fable, or proverb. The rim, in turn, is often ringed with the letters of the alphabet.

Mugs were treated as another medium for instructive messages. They were often inscribed with such inspirational phrases as "Industry Is Fortune's Handmaiden," with religious verses, rhymes, and poems, or with such dedications as "For a Good Child."

Designed especially for children, the 19th-century English and American mugs above are about three inches high; the children's plates at right range from four to six inches in diameter.

GLOSSARY OF POTTERY AND PORCELAIN

◆ *agateware* A kind of Staffordshire pottery made to imitate agate stone. Agateware is characterized by a marbled or veined appearance, achieved by blending clays of different color in the body of a piece (for solid agateware) or by blending slips of different color on the surface of a piece (for surface agateware). Both types were used for tableware; solid agateware was also used for figurines.

agateware

◆ *biscuit* or *bisque* Unglazed pottery or porcelain that has been fired only once.

◆ *blue-and-white porcelain* A term for white porcelain decorated in underglaze blue. Blue-and-white porcelain was first developed in China, possibly as early as the 8th century. After it was duplicated in England around 1750, the process for making this pottery was commonly used in that country. Canton, Nanking, Fitzhugh, and Blue Willow are patterns used on blue-and-white porcelain.

◆ *Blue Willow* The name for a popular china pattern that originated in England in the 1760s but has also been used widely in America. Based on Chinese export porcelain patterns, it features a willow tree, an orange tree, a teahouse, and a bridge. The Blue Willow pattern appears on tableware made from many ceramic bodies, including ironstone and bone china.

Blue Willow

◆ *body* The composite material from which ceramics are made.

◆ *bone china* A soft-paste porcelain, made with animal-bone ash, that has been the standard type of English porcelain since the early 19th century.

◆ *canary luster* A rare type of lusterware characterized by a bright yellow background color and often decorated with transfer prints.

◆ *Canton* One of the most commonly used patterns on Chinese export porcelain. Painted in underglaze blue, it features a stylized Chinese landscape and, often, a scalloped border. Porcelain decorated in the Canon pattern was imported directly from China to America from about 1785 into the 20th century.

◆ *ceramics* The general term for all objects made of fired clay.

◆ *china* A common term for porcelain. The name derives from "china ware," which referred to the porcelain that Europeans imported from China beginning in the Middle Ages.

◆ *Chinese export porcelain* A type of hard-paste porcelain made in China between the 1500s and 1800s specifically for export to Europe and America. Typical patterns include floral, scenic, and armorial designs. Nearly all of the early Chinese export porcelain was blue and white; by the early 1700s, green decoration was used, as were red-and-gold patterns.

◆ *creamware* A type of cream-colored earthenware with a transparent lead glaze that was first produced around 1760 in Staffordshire, England. Made of white clay mixed with flint, creamware was popularized by Josiah Wedgwood, an English potter. It was renamed Queen's ware in 1765 after Wedgwood secured an order from Queen Charlotte for a dinnerware set in creamware.

◆ *delftware* The term for tin-glazed earthenware made in Holland beginning in the second half of the 16th century, and soon after in England. Commonly, delftware was made in imitation of blue-and-white Chinese porcelain. However, the best 17th-

delftware

century pieces were produced with polychrome decoration, and much English delftware made in the 18th century combined one or more colors with blue.

◆ *earthenware* The term for any porous pottery that must be glazed to be impervious to liquids. Redware, faience, delftware, and creamware are types of earthenware.

◆ *faience* The French term meaning brightly colored, decorated tin-glazed earthenware. The name derives from Faenza, an Italian pottery center that produced wares popular in France in the 16th century. Faience was used for dishes, figurines, and display pieces.

◆ *Fitzhugh* A rather ornate pattern used on Chinese export porcelain that features pomegranates, butterflies, emblems, and flowers on a diamond-patterned background. Named for an English family involved in the Chinese export business, the Fitzhugh pattern was used as both a border and central decoration. It appeared primarily in underglaze blue, but also in green, orange, or brown.

◆ *Flow Blue* A term used to describe ironstone, stoneware, or porcelain decorated with a colored underglaze that diffused or "flowed" during the firing, causing the patterns to blur

Flow Blue

slightly. The technique was developed around 1820. While cobalt blue was the first color used and remained the

most common, pieces can also be found with brown, green, and mulberry-colored underglaze decoration. Flow Blue was used for inexpensive tablewares and personal accessories, such as basins and pitchers.

◆ *Gaudy Dutch* A type of Staffordshire earthenware decorated in underglaze blue and overglaze enamel, and made for export to the Pennsylvania Germans from 1810 to 1830.

Gaudy Dutch

Gaudy Dutch is characterized by vivid floral patterns designed to imitate the look of Imari. Typical colors used in the patterns include pink, yellow, green, and red. Gaudy Dutch decoration was used mainly for plates and tea sets.

◆ *Gaudy Welsh* A type of decorated porcelain characterized by gay floral patterns painted in enamel and detailed with copper luster or gilding. It was made in Swansea, Wales, for export to America between 1830 and 1845 and used mainly for tea sets.

◆ *glaze* A glass-like coating, usually made from feldspar, lead, or tin, and any of various metallic oxides for color, that is fired onto ceramics.

◆ *hard-paste* or *true porcelain* A delicate, translucent porcelain that was first made in China in the 7th century and duplicated in Europe in 1708. The paste, or body, is made principally

from kaolin and petuntze, or china stone.

◆ *historical ware* One of several terms for transfer-printed Staffordshire decorated with American historical figures and scenes. Introduced in the 1820s, it was made in England expressly for export to the United States. The vast majority of patterns, including the first, were designed in blue, but by the middle of the 19th century, pink, green, and brown patterns had also appeared. Historical ware is also known as Historical Blue or Old Blue.

◆ *Imari* A type of porcelain made in Arita, Japan, and shipped through the port of Imari to Europe beginning in the 1600s. Imari is characterized by floral patterns in underglaze blue and overglaze red and gold. English and European imitations of these patterns were extremely popular in the 19th century.

ironstone

◆ *ironstone* A durable white pottery patented in Staffordshire in 1813 and widely produced in America from 1860 to 1900. Used mainly for tableware, it was known by a variety of names, including hotel china and semiporcelain.

◆ *jaspé* A type of decorated redware produced primarily from the 1700s to the 1930s by French potters in the Alsace region. Decoration includes mottled glazes, polka dots, and simple bird and flower motifs. Jaspé was used mainly for kitchenware.

◆ *kaolin* A very pure white clay also known as china clay.

◆ *lusterware* A type of pottery made primarily in England in the 1800s and characterized by a metallic finish in a gold, copper, pink, lilac, or, rarely, yellow color. The luster finish might cover an entire piece or be combined with hand-painted designs or transfer prints. Lusterware was used mainly for tea sets and display pieces.

◆ *maiolica* Tin-glazed earthenware made in Italy primarily during the Renaissance. The name derives from the Italian word for wares imported from Majorca, Spain.

◆ *majolica* Lead-glazed earthenware molded in various naturalistic forms such as those of fruits, fish, and

majolica

animals, and decorated in bright, semitransparent colors including bottle green, pink, yellow, cobalt blue, and turquoise. Majolica was made from the mid- to late 19th century in England and America and was typically used for plates, platters, and pitchers. The name derives from

maiolica but the glazes are not related.

◆ *mochaware* A type of decorated earthenware made primarily in England from the 1780s to the 1850s. Decoration includes a fernlike pattern, a squiggly "worm" design, and a "cat's-eye" motif—in blue, gray, brown, green, ocher, and black glazes. Pieces decorated with colored bands are also known as banded creamware. Mochaware was used primarily for mugs, bowls, and pitchers.

mochaware

◆ *Nanking* A pattern applied in underglaze blue and used on fine quality Chinese export porcelain. It features a stylized Oriental landscape. Although similar to Canton, Nanking is more finely painted and incorporates a gold rim.

◆ *overglaze* An enamel decoration that is fired onto a ceramic piece that has already been glazed and fired; it may be transfer-printed or hand-painted.

◆ *porcelain* A hard and translucent, glasslike ceramic that usually has a white body and produces a ringing sound when struck. The three primary types of porcelain are hard-paste, soft-paste, and bone china.

◆ *pottery* The general term for all ceramics without exception. The term, however, is often used for all ceramic wares except porcelain.

◆ *Prattware* A lead-glazed earthenware with a lightweight, cream-colored body first made around 1775 in Staffordshire by the potter William Pratt. Prattware is characterized by a combination of underglaze colors—usually ocher, blue, and green—and relief decoration. Prattware was used for jugs, oval plaques, and figurines.

◆ *redware* A type of lead-glazed pottery made from a number of coarse, porous clays that vary in color but are all reddish when fired. Redware was made in America primarily from the 17th through the early 20th century. It may be decorated with incising or impressed patterns; with colored slip—usually in yellow or black—applied in wavy lines, abstract patterns, or words; with solid-color lead glazes in brown; or with sgraffito. A utility pottery, redware was used for tableware, jugs, jars, and pots.

◆ *Rockingham* A type of pottery—usually yellowware—decorated with a brown glaze characterized by a mottled, tortoiseshell-like appearance. Rockingham was made in England and in more than sixty American potteries from the mid-1800s until around 1900. It was typically used for kitchenware, mugs, pitchers, teapots, and display pieces.

Rockingham

◆ *sgraffito* A decorative technique that involves coating pottery with a thin layer of slip before glazing, then scratching or incising a design in the slip to reveal the body of the pottery piece underneath. A similar effect may also be achieved by incising through the glaze. Used both in the East and the West, the process was extremely widespread. The most notable examples of sgraffito are found on pieces of 18th- and early-19th-century Pennsylvania-German redware.

sgraffito

◆ *slip* A clay thinned with water to a semiliquid state.

◆ *soft-paste* or *artificial porcelain* A type of porcelain that is made from kaolin mixed with soapstone, ground glass, bone ash, or any of the other materials used as substitutes for the china stone in hard-paste porcelain.

◆ *spatterware* A type of English pottery made for export from 1820 to 1850, decorated with tiny (usually uniform) dots of color applied with a sponge or rag, or spattered on with a brush. The decoration is finer and more precise than that on spongeware and is often combined with hand-painted motifs. Decoration also includes sponged motifs in the shapes of hearts and flowers. The most com-

mon colors are blue or red applied to a white background. Spatterware was typically used for platters, pitchers, and teacups.

spongeware

◆ *spongeware* Any type of pottery— usually one with a heavy body— whose decoration has been dabbed on with a sponge or other soft material. The patterns, which are generally cruder than the fine decoration on spatterware, are typically in blue, brown, or green. Common in America after the 1890s, spongeware was generally used for utilitarian pieces, such as pitchers and crocks.

◆ *Staffordshire* A general term for the wares produced in Staffordshire, a county in central England that became a major pottery and porcelain center in the mid-1600s.

◆ *stoneware* The term for a hard pottery made of clay and fusible stone that was widely used in England and America beginning in the 1600s. Stoneware is often fired with a salt glaze that creates a slightly pitted surface. The body color may be white, gray, or brown, and decoration includes incised or painted motifs such as trees, flowers, and birds, usually detailed in cobalt blue. Stoneware was typically used for pitchers, bottles, and crocks.

◆ *Sunderland* A type of lusterware characterized by a mottled pink luster

that might be combined with transfer-print decoration. Patterns typically incorporate sailing ships and sentimental verses. The name derives from the English town where much of the lusterware with this type of decoration was first produced in the early 1800s.

◆ *tin-glazed earthenware* Any earthenware covered with a tin oxide glaze to create an opaque white surface; usually decorated with blue and other colors. Maiolica, faience, and delftware are types of tin-glazed earthenware.

◆ *transfer print* A type of decoration in which an engraved picture is transferred from a copper plate by means of paper to the surface of a piece of pottery, either under or over the glaze.

◆ *underglaze* A colored decoration made from a metal oxide applied to a ceramic before a clear glaze is fired on. Cobalt blue is the color most commonly used and is generally referred to as underglaze blue.

yellowware

◆ *yellowware* A type of earthenware that ranges in color from pale straw to deep yellow when fired, and is often decorated with colored bands. Made in America primarily from the 1830s into the early 1900s, yellowware was considered ovenproof and was typically used for casserole dishes and other bakeware.

American Glass

The tablewares above, made in clear glass and in cranberry, were produced in the early 19th century by blowing molten glass into patterned molds. This process, which required skilled handcraftsmanship, was the forerunner to machine-molding of glass.

Patented in the 1820s, machine-pressed glass revolutionized the glass industry and helped make inexpensive glassware available to the average American household. Prior to the invention of pressed glass, glassmaking involved blowing the material into a mold, or blowing glass freeform and cutting or etching it by hand. Pressed glass was made by forcing molten glass into a mold with a mechanical plunger. The process allowed manufacturers to reproduce the same patterns repeatedly, and by the 1850s it was used to make the majority of glassware in this country.

The first designs, known as lacy glass, fea-tured hundreds of tiny facets and were intended to imitate the look and sparkle of expensive hand-cut glass. Early pieces of lacy glass are heavy and brilliant and produce a bell-like ring when they are struck.

After 1840, pressed glass became simpler in design and was known as pattern glass because the same pattern was used for an entire set of tableware. While lacy glass was made only in individual pieces, pattern-glass sets—in some three hundred patterns—included plates and bowls and such "extras" as butter dishes, sugar bowls, creamers, and compotes. Collectors find it a challenge to assemble a complete set.

The pressed glass opposite dates from the mid- to late 1800s. Fierce competition among makers and the Victorian taste for ornament resulted in a broad range of designs.

Patterns in Pressed Glass

A Beehive lacy glass dessert plate, a Westward Ho creamer, and a Coin pitcher.

In 1827, when Deming Jarves, the owner of the Boston & Sandwich Glass Company, first used the new technology of machine-pressing glass to produce a tumbler, his employees were so fearful for their jobs that they threatened him with bodily harm. Jarves retreated to his house for six weeks, but machine-made glass had arrived.

Indeed, pressed glass continued to be popular until the early 20th century. Early pieces, made from about 1830 to 1850, are known as lacy glass for their delicate, intricate look. Lacy glass patterns are characterized by a background of small raised dots and often feature Gothic arches or the swags and eagles favored in the Empire period. Most lacy glass was de-signed as individual pieces rather than as sets.

More widely available to collectors is the pressed glass made after 1840, known as pattern glass. Illustrated opposite are twelve of the hundreds of pattern glass designs made. In general, these patterns fall into three periods: from about 1840 to 1870, simplified geometrics were favored; from about 1865 to about 1880, both abstract patterns and realistic depictions of animals, human figures, birds, and plants appeared; and by the late 19th century a diverse range of patterns, including some "lacy" revivals and designs with historical themes, were popular.

Manufacturers of pressed glass gave each pattern a name, such as Comet, Pioneer, Ribbon Candy, and Dewdrop with Star, that tended to reflect its design. Over time, a number of these pattern names changed: Comet, for example became known as Horn of Plenty, and Pioneer, which features a buffalo and a pioneer's log cabin set against a backdrop of mountains, is today referred to as Westward Ho. Once called Silver Age, the pattern now known as Coin incorporates actual impressions of American coins. This pattern was reportedly made for only five months in 1892 in anticipation of the World's Columbian Exposition in Chicago; the United States government put a stop to its manufacture on the grounds that it violated counterfeiting laws.

EARLY GEOMETRIC PATTERNS c. 1840-1870

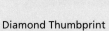

Diamond Thumbprint

Horn of Plenty

New England Pineapple

Sawtooth

NATURALISTIC AND ABSTRACT PATTERNS c. 1865-1880

Dewdrop with Star

Wildflower

Bellflower, Double Vine

Ribbon Candy

LATE-19TH- AND EARLY-20TH-CENTURY PATTERNS c. 1875-1910

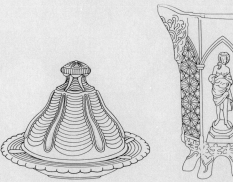

Ribbed Drape

Classic

Garfield Drape

Daisy and Button, Crossbar

107

Milk Glass

Milk glass in the Cosmos pattern, above, is distinguished by painted detail intended to emphasize the molded design. Produced by glasshouses in Fostoria, Ohio, and Coraopolis, Pennsylvania, it was made primarily between 1894 and 1915.

Milk glass is a type of opaque glass made to imitate porcelain. Depending on the amount of tin added to the molten glass mixture, this glass can range in color from a streaky alabaster to a dense chalk white. Milk glass was originally made by hand and was not mass-produced until the late 1800s; it is the Victorian-era wares that are most popular today.

Inexpensive tableware made of milk glass includes bowls, compotes, pitchers, and tureens. Covered, animal-shape dishes and plates that feature a lattice rim and a painted flower or bird in the center are sought after. Typical decoration includes sawtooth, stipple, and floral patterns. One of the most popular painted patterns was Cosmos, characterized by pastel-colored flowers.

Now known as milk glass, pieces like those at left were originally called opalware by some makers.

Variegated Glassware

The variegated glassware at right includes purple slag glass, also known as marble glass, and brown chocolate glass. Nearly all chocolate glass was made by the Indiana Tumbler and Goblet Company from 1900 until 1903, when the factory burned down.

A novelty among Victorian pressed-glass collectibles is variegated glassware, distinguished by a swirled, marblelike pattern. One type, known as slag glass, was made by combining colored glass with milk glass; purple was the color most commonly used. Slag glass was produced in both America and England in the late 1800s. The largest manufacturer in America was the Pennsylvania firm of Chal-linor, Taylor & Company, but pieces made by this and other American companies are generally unmarked. English slag glass, by contrast, usually bears the maker's mark.

A rare type of variegated glassware is chocolate glass, produced primarily by the Indiana Tumbler and Goblet Company in Greentown, Indiana, at the turn of the century. Just how chocolate glass was made is now a mystery.

CARING FOR GLASS

Whether antique or new, fine glassware requires gentle care. Because heat and excessive changes in temperature can cause glass to crack, any glassware that you value should be washed by hand, not in a dishwasher. It is a good idea to place a towel in the bottom of the sink, or to use a plastic dishpan, so that the glass will not chip if you drop it. Wash one piece at a time using lukewarm water and a mild detergent. Rinse with clean, tepid water, or a weak solution of vinegar and water; the latter will help prevent spotting. A linen dishcloth is the best choice for drying most glass because it will not leave traces of lint.

If you are washing very fragile glass, do not immerse the pieces in water. Instead, wipe them clean with a damp linen cloth. Avoid using a dry cloth, which can cause tiny scratches on delicate pieces.

When washing a piece that has a stopper or top, such as a decanter or sugar bowl, it is important to allow both parts to dry thoroughly before replacing the top. If moisture is trapped inside a glass container, the piece can turn cloudy. This condition is known as glass sickness. Because the trapped moisture actually causes the surface of the glass to break down, glass sickness causes irreversible damage.

Other types of discoloration, however—such as stains from red wine or cut flowers—can be treated successfully. Some stains can be removed by washing the glass with fresh lemon juice, a weak solution of ammonia and water, or vinegar diluted with water.

To clean stains in hard-to-reach places, such as the interior of a vase or decanter, pour in a little dry rice, then fill the piece with water and shake gently. You can also try filling the piece with water and adding a denture-cleaning tablet.

When packing glass for storage, make sure the pieces are completely dry before wrapping them. Because paper can absorb and retain moisture, it is safest to wrap glass in plastic: bubble-wrap works well. Stoppers and lids should be removed and wrapped separately. Choose a carton that can be closed on top, and be sure not to pack the box too tightly. Store the carton in a closet or room that will remain cool and dry.

The salt cellars at right reveal the diversity of materials and forms that distinguish these small tablewares. These pieces— from England, America, Germany, and France—date from the mid-1800s to the early 1900s and are made of silver, ceramic, pewter, and glass. The collection includes simple bowls, as well as fancy novelty designs such as a bird's nest, a mermaid and shell, a sleigh, and a swan.

112

Salt Cellars

Until salt shakers became popular in America in the late 19th century, salt was served at the table in bowls called salt cellars, dishes, dips, or, simply, salts. The custom of using such salt cellars had been practiced in Europe for many centuries. The earliest types were large, communal salts placed in the center of the table. According to a medieval tradition, guests were seated near the host "above the salt," whereas children and social inferiors sat "below" it. Small, individual salt cellars were first made in the 1600s but did not replace communal salts until the late 1800s.

Pewter salts were probably made by most 18th-century American pewterers, but few examples remain. Among the pewter pieces found today are small, chalicelike salts, often decorated with a beaded rim, and small dishes, sometimes lined with colored glass. Because dinnerware sets seldom included salts, ceramic pieces are also rare, although some have been made in lusterware, faience, and mochaware.

The most commonly available salts are made of glass. Blown-glass salts, in fact, were among the first wares made in colonial glasshouses. Pressed-glass pieces began to replace those of blown glass in the 1820s. In addition to the usual dish or bowl type, often designed to match a table service, glass salts are available in many novelty shapes, including miniature animals, shoes, carriages, and boats. While most of the glass salts found today are "open," a few rare pieces exist with covers.

Vintage Clothing

F avorites among the antique textiles collected today are modest dresses, skirts,
trousers, shirts, aprons, and bonnets
from the 1800s that were typically worn by farm
and working-class families. These handmade
garments, of homespun linen, cotton, and wool,
were plain and practical. While such clothing
might reflect the influence of fashion with a high
bodice or short sleeves, it was usually generously
cut and had few embellishments other than
smocking or simple embroidery. Because cloth
was so valuable, clothing was often worn until it
was threadbare, and vintage country apparel is
often found with patches and other repairs.

Because of their small size, children's garments from the period have a particular charm
for collectors. Dresses and tunics were worn by
both girls and boys, and boys also dressed
in blousy smocks, overalls, and trousers with
fronts that could be buttoned onto their shirts.

Nineteenth-century garments of homespun cotton
hang at left along with Amish hats.

The mid-19th-century
children's dresses above,
from Pennsylvania, were
handmade of red and white
checked cotton. The dress on
the left has been repaired
(as is typical of antique
clothing) with a patch on
one sleeve. The dress on
the right features hand-
stitched smocking, often
found on country
garments.

Early Mirrors

Imported from Europe, the earliest mirrors used in the colonies were considered a luxury since glass was expensive. The glass used in mirrors was backed with reflective tin and set in simple frames. In the 1700s the colonists began crafting their own mirrors using imported glass, and these too were primarily utilitarian in appearance. The only decoration might be a crest or scroll along the top edge of the frame. Some crested mirrors were known as courting mirrors; tradition has it that they were given to women by their suitors.

More elaborate looking glasses were available, however, for those who could afford them. Frames were often adorned with carving, paint, inlay, gilding, veneer, or other ornament similar to that found on furniture. The glass itself might also be decorated—with painting or engraving.

While most early mirrors are square or rectangular, there are also round, oval, and lyre-shaped examples. In addition to wall mirrors, hand mirrors and standing "dressing glasses" (made for shaving or to be set on vanity tables) are popular among collectors.

This collection of wall and hand mirrors includes simple pieces from the 18th and 19th centuries. All were made in America and have their original frames. Such mirrors are typically small, because the glass plates were often made from cylinders— which had to be cut and flattened—rather than from glass sheets.

123

Hatboxes and Bandboxes

Particularly popular in the 19th century, hatboxes and bandboxes were not only used to store a variety of personal belongings at home, but also served as luggage. Made of pasteboard or wood, these lightweight paper-covered boxes came in countless shapes and sizes.

Because hats were an important accessory in the wardrobes of both men and women—and were often made of costly furs or silk—they were highly valued and carefully protected when not in use. Found in America as early as the 1600s, storage boxes for hats were shaped to accommodate particular styles, including colonial-era tricorns, the accordion-pleated bonnets known as calashes worn in the late 1700s, and the silk hoods and towering top hats that were fashionable in the 1800s.

Bandboxes were first made in the 18th century to hold the men's collarbands then in vogue. The inexpensive containers were soon adopted by women to store ribbons, jewelry, and clothing. They reached their height of popularity in the 1830s and 1840s.

Both hatboxes and bandboxes are distinguished by their coverings: colorful hand-decorated or machine-printed papers. Many of the papers were actual pieces of wallpaper; others were designed specifically to decorate the boxes. The most coveted paper designs incorporate historical scenes and landmarks, or commemorate famous events.

The display of paper-covered bandboxes at left includes 19th-century pieces as well as contemporary boxes made by the owner. The small boxes probably held lace or patches for patchwork quilts; elongated boxes stored tortoise-shell combs.

AUNT HANNAH'S BANDBOXES

Hannah Davis, a New Hampshire spinster who became widely known as Aunt Hannah, was one of the foremost makers of bandboxes in the 19th century. Aunt Hannah made her boxes by hand and, in spite of competition from large bandbox and wallpaper manufacturers, created a successful cottage industry that flourished between the 1820s and 1850s.

Because Aunt Hannah's boxes were so sturdy and so well constructed, they have outlasted those fabricated by her competitors and are now prized by collectors. Instead of using pasteboard, as most commercial boxmakers did, Aunt Hannah crafted wooden boxes with spruce sides and pine lids and bottoms. A clockmaker's daughter, she was adept at woodworking and invented a machine that could slice logs into extremely thin pieces.

To obtain paper for covering the boxes, Aunt Hannah bartered with her neighbors: in return for finished bandboxes, friends gladly provided the craftswoman with newspapers—used for the linings—and pieces of colorful wallpaper. Her boxes are known for their blue wallpaper with floral designs, and for scenic papers depicting episodes from the life of Napoleon. Each was marked with her trademark—a label in one of ten different designs that carried the inscription "Warranted Nailed Bandboxes, Made by Hannah Davis."

Driving a sleigh throughout the winter months and a wagon the rest of the year, Aunt Hannah peddled her wares to the mill girls working in New England textile factories. During lunch hour, the young women swarmed around her, eager to surrender their wages for new bandboxes. The prices ranged from twelve to fifty cents.

c. 1825

The covering on this bandbox, which pictures duck hunters, is one of the few scenic papers used by Hannah Davis.

c. 1840

This Hannah Davis bandbox features wallpaper printed with a swan-handled fruit basket and foliage.

c. 1844

Pineapples—a traditional symbol of hospitality—pattern the wallpaper used in this band-box made by Aunt Hannah.

Used for washing, basins and pitchers like the pottery pieces above were household necessities before indoor plumbing became common around the end of the 19th century. Pitchers and basins in early chamber sets were quite small but became larger as time went on.

Before bathrooms became common in the late 1800s, a washstand was traditionally placed in each bedroom to hold a chamber set—a pitcher to carry water and a basin for washing. While such sets were used widely from the 1700s onward—daily washing was not a common practice in earlier times—most found today date from the 1800s to the early 1900s.

Early chamber sets were limited to the wash-basin and pitcher, but by the mid-1800s the inexpensive pottery sets being produced in quantity by European and American makers generally came complete with a soap dish, sponge dish, toothbrush holder and cup, slop pail (for discarded water), and chamber pot. Such sets were available in plain white ironstone or with painted or transfer-printed designs that matched on all the pieces. Floral motifs and gold trim were popular stock decorations. Special orders were also possible; a set might be custom-designed, for example, to match the wallpaper in a bedroom.

While soap dishes, or soap boxes, came with many chamber sets, they were also sold separately. First used in the mid-1700s, they generally had a lid and a pierced drainer and were designed to preserve soap by keeping it as dry as possible when not in use. Soap dishes were made in many materials, including silver, hardwood, glass, and, of course, pottery.

Chamber Sets

The late-19th- and early-20th-century soap dishes at left were made in England and America; pottery and porcelain were the favored materials during that period. Often decorated with molded or underglaze designs, such pieces are generally found in round, oval, and rectangular shapes.

Writing Collectibles

The embroidered wallet above once belonged to John Vicary, a wealthy sea captain who lived in Philadelphia in the 1700s. The documents surrounding it were found inside, and include a household inventory, bills for his daughter's education, and an order for his wife's casket.

Collectibles that have to do with writing include desk boxes as well as the interesting accouterments associated with them: pens and pencils, paper clips, inkwells, blotters, stamp and document boxes, letters, diaries, deeds, and record books.

Before the 1700s, "desk" referred to a wooden box used to hold writing materials and books. This portable box, usually made with a hinged front, was eventually placed on a stand and evolved into the first stationary desk—the desk-on-frame—which appeared around 1700. Still in use, the portable desk boxes then became known as lap or field desks, and were widely used in the 19th century by itinerant professionals, such as ministers and lawyers. Once stationary desks became more common, desk organizers and stationery racks became fashionable for the desk top.

During the late 18th and the 19th centuries no well-equipped desk top was complete without an inkwell. Ink was usually made by a chemist and sold in apothecaries and bookshops, or

Continued

The display at left features a portable stationery box with ivory-handled accessories and a silver-trimmed oak cabinet with two inkwells; both are English and date from the turn of the century. Other pieces include tea caddies and salesmen's furniture samples, now often used as desk accessories.

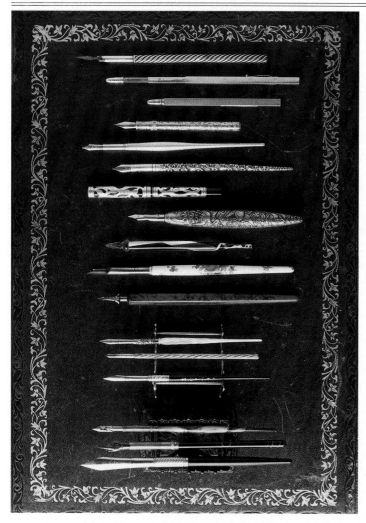

The English and American writing implements above left were made between the late 1800s and early 1900s. They include fountain and dip pens and mechanical pencils. The paper clips above right are the large, spring-loaded type used in Victorian times. The rare boar's head clip at top left has a bristle pen wipe.

mixed from a powder at home. Prepared ink was stored in capped ink bottles until needed; it was then transferred from a master bottle to a well, which served as a shallow reservoir for dipping pens. Inkwells ranged from simple pots to lavishly decorated pieces mounted on silver bases or painted with the owner's coat of arms. They were often part of a desk set (also known as an inkstand, stand, or standish), a popular accessory in the 1700s and 1800s. An inkstand usually comprised a tray with an inkwell, a penholder, a seal, a sealing wax pot, a candle for melting the wax, and a caster, which was used for sprinkling sand to blot wet ink.

Early writing implements are equally diverse.

Quill pens were widely used until the latter half of the 19th century, when steel pens, first produced commercially in 1858 in Camden, New Jersey, began to replace them. These were followed by pens made of gold, silver, or brass. Other welcome additions to the desk top were mechanical pencils with retractable leads, invented around 1830. Novelties include pen and pencil combinations and a kind of telescoping pencil that extended to become a ruler.

Paper clips could also be elaborate: spring-loaded Victorian pieces were often made in whimsical shapes such as hands or animals, or designed as portraits of famous people; some were lavishly ornamented.

The inkstands and inkwells opposite, ranging from large porcelain and glass pieces to tiny traveling wells made of wood, display various designs popular in the 1800s.

CARING FOR PAPER

Nearly everyone owns old documents, letters, or photographs that might have historical value as a collection or sentimental value as family mementos. As do other collectibles, such papers require proper care if they are to be preserved. Fortunately, it is possible to display and even handle papers and photographs safely if you take certain precautions.

Anyone who has pulled a box of crumbling brown letters from an attic or a stash of mildewed photographs from a basement knows that there are better places to store old papers. Indeed, heat, moisture, dust, and insects are among the worst enemies of paper. Extreme heat speeds the aging process of paper by drying it out and causing it to crack and discolor. Do not store pieces in an area where temperatures are high or display them near a radiator or fireplace.

Excessive humidity tends to cause rust-colored mildew spots, called foxing, to appear on paper, and will in time cause the paper fibers to deteriorate. In many cases, foxing can be removed by experts, but it can reappear if the paper piece is exposed

to moisture again. A humidity level of 30 to 50 percent is ideal for photographs, and 50 to 70 percent is best for other papers. Good air circulation also reduces the risk of mildew and mold. Make sure that in framing, papers and photographs are separated from the glass with a mat to prevent build-up of moisture; and avoid hanging pictures on damp outer walls.

Keeping your papers and photographs clean is equally important. By using the appropriate storage and display materials (see the following pages), you can prevent dust from becoming imbedded in paper fibers and keep insects such as silverfish, woodworms, and termites, which feed on cellulose and glue, from lunching on your collection.

Light is another concern. Even indirect sunlight will dry out paper, and can cause ink, color printing, and photographic images—as well as the paper itself—to fade. If papers are particularly valuable, it is wise to handle them in bright light only when necessary. And if you display these important pieces, never place them directly opposite a window.

Old papers and photographs like those at left are fragile and easily damaged. Properly cared for, however, they can last for generations.

CONSERVATION OF DOCUMENTS AND PHOTOGRAPHS

Recommended supplies for the home archivist include acid-free envelopes and protective albums.

Because handling can damage paper documents and photographs, it is best to protect your pieces before you do so. Fortunately, there are many archival products designed for this purpose, and they are readily available from mail-order companies or from art-supply stores. Such products, which include albums, envelopes, tissue, and mat board, are made with acid-free materials to prevent papers from turning brown or deteriorating.

Two types of archival supplies that are commonly used for storing individual documents and photographs are acid-free paper envelopes and archival-quality plastic enclosures.

The envelopes are useful because they protect their contents against light and do not retain moisture. However, because such envelopes are opaque, the paper stored inside must still be removed each time it is examined.

A good alternative is an enclosure made of clear plastic Mylar or triacetate film. Ready-made sleeves and folders are available; you can also buy the plastic film and make your own sealed envelopes in a process known as encapsulation (see the directions opposite).

Encapsulation involves sandwiching a document between two pieces of the plastic film, which are then

sealed with a special double-sided tape known as film tape; a small gap is left at one corner so that moisture will not build up inside. The document is held in place by static electricity. The procedure is simple to learn, but it may require a little practice to keep the plastic film and the document aligned while you are taping. Properly executed, it will allow the safe handling of even fragile pieces. (Encapsulation should not, however, be used for works in pastel or any art medium that can lift or smudge.) To provide maximum protection for valuable papers, it is wise to have them deacidified by a specialist before encapsulating them.

A. Plastic paperweight is centered on document to keep it from shifting.

B. Tape should be placed on Mylar with ends butting neatly.

C. Squeegee should be pulled toward gap to remove air from envelope.

D. Starting at corners, backing is carefully peeled from film tape.

MATERIALS

The directions for encapsulation below call for Mylar polyester film, which is available in 24 x 36-inch sheets and comes in several weights. Be sure the Mylar you choose is heavy enough to support the document that is to be encapsulated. Mylar in a 3- or 4-milligram weight is recommended for small, light documents; Mylar in a 5-milligram weight can be used for larger, heavier pieces. Never use shrink wrap or polyvinyl chloride to encapsulate documents.

• 2 sheets Mylar polyester film •
• Large sheet graph paper • Double-sided film tape •
• Lint-free cloth • Plastic paperweight •
• Small squeegee • Hard-rubber brayer (roller) •
• Measuring tape •
• Scissors •

DIRECTIONS

1. Using scissors, cut two sheets of Mylar film to measure 2 inches wider and 2 inches longer than dimensions of document or other paper you wish to encapsulate.

2. Center one sheet of Mylar film on graph paper and align. Wipe surface of film with lint-free cloth to remove dust and increase static charge.

3. Center document on top of Mylar sheet, allowing 1-inch margin on each edge and aligning with graph paper underneath.

4. Place paperweight in center of document to hold it in position (Illustration A).

5. Measure along one side of document and cut piece of tape to same length; leave protective backing on tape intact. Leaving about a ¼-inch margin between tape and document, align tape with graph paper and document and press sticky side onto Mylar. Repeat for two adjacent sides of document, carefully butting ends of tape at corners with no overlap (Illustration B).

6. Measure untaped side of document, and cut tape ¹⁄₁₆ inch shorter than measurement. Apply tape as above, butting ends at one corner and leaving gap at other corner.

7. Wipe one side of second sheet of Mylar with lint-free cloth. Remove paperweight from document and place second sheet of Mylar, clean side down, so that it aligns with bottom sheet of Mylar. Carefully holding layers in place, pull squeegee over them toward gap to force out as much air as possible (Illustration C). Replace paperweight.

8. At corner opposite gap, lift top sheet of Mylar at corner. Starting at that corner, carefully peel paper backing from tape along one side of document. Let corner drop back into place and pull squeegee over Mylar to affix tape. Starting at same corner, repeat process for adjacent side. Repeat for two remaining sides of document (Illustration D), pulling squeegee toward gap.

9. Remove paperweight and roll brayer over layers to seal tightly.

10. Using scissors, trim edges of Mylar film, leaving ⅛-inch margin around edge of tape.

The rabbit collectibles above are natural additions to a children's room. Some of the stuffed bunnies are still dressed in clothing that was handmade generations ago.

more cats—toys, advertising memorabilia, and games. The cat theme is continued by two hooked rugs made in the 1930s, a 19th-century Tennessee quilt with cat appliqués, and other cat furnishings, such as the calling card stand and the small iron doorstop next to the settee.

The homeowners also favor items with rabbit motifs, which were usually intended specifically for the young. Among the rabbit collectibles that they have displayed in the children's room above are a child's hooked rug, pull toys, and stuffed bunnies. "These animals have humor and history—and almost human traits," say the collectors. "Our whole family enjoys them; they make our house come alive."

Tips on Collecting

Long-time collectors agree that the only real rule in collecting is to buy the things you will enjoy owning. Most of the fun is in the search. Whether you have a small collection you want to expand, or are starting from scratch, there are many places to look.

The classified sections in most newspapers include advertisements for auctions, flea markets, and regional antiques shows. Also listed are estate sales, in which the contents of a home (and sometimes a barn) are sold; often it is at these sales that the most interesting items turn up.

It is best to arrive at a show or sale at the opening hour, before the merchandise has been picked over. Auctions are usually preceded by "previewing" hours, and it is wise to attend. The preview will give you time to look over and handle items, and decide how much you want to spend. Never buy a piece at auction unless you have examined it carefully first: cracks and replaced parts will not be readily visible when the piece is on the auction block.

Developing a discerning eye not only will help you improve the quality of your collections but also can contribute to your enjoyment of the pursuit and ownership of the pieces. Attending shows "just to look" allows you to compare prices and judge value. At shows and in shops, be sure to ask questions about objects that interest you. If the dealer is knowledgeable, he can tell you something about the history and special characteristics of a piece. Such information will increase your expertise and help you understand some of the mysteries of collecting—such as why two similar-looking pieces can sell for very different prices.

Also helpful are the many paperback price guides that are published annually, covering everything from comic books to fine porcelain. When using a price guide, make sure you have the most up-to-date edition, and keep in mind that the prices listed should be considered as guidelines only.

You may also want to check your library for trade publications and recent books on a particular subject. By reading, and by visiting museums and historical societies, you will give yourself the chance to look at and learn from the best examples.

THE STORY OF STEIFF

First made in the 1880s in the small West German town of Giengen, Steiff toys have been loved by children—and adults—ever since. The familiar dolls, teddy bears, and other stuffed animals are never really outgrown, and vintage examples are avidly sought by collectors throughout America and Europe.

The Steiff company was named for its founder, Margarete Steiff, and is still run in Giengen by family members today. Born in 1847, Steiff contracted polio as a child, and was left paralyzed in her legs and right arm. Although confined to a wheelchair, she was able to master the use of a sewing machine, and opened a clothing shop for women and children in 1877.

During her first year in business, Steiff made a pincushion for herself in the form of an elephant, using materials from her uncle's felt factory. The elephant was so popular with local children that she made other animals—monkeys, bears, and horses—as gifts. In 1880 one of her brothers took a bundle of the toys to a country fair and sold them all. Soon, Steiff's business began to shift from clothing to toys.

In 1893, the first Steiff toy catalog appeared. By then, various members of her family had joined Steiff in the business. The company's inventory of stuffed toys, made of felt and vel-vet, included dolls, clowns, and animals such as sheep, mice, and apes (as well as elephants).

The Steiff company did not attain international fame, however, until after 1897, when Margarete Steiff's nephews became involved in production and sales. One nephew, Richard Steiff, designed the first Steiff bear, based on sketches he had made of bear cubs at the Stuttgart Zoo. A prototype was made, standing twenty-two inches tall, with mohair plush for the fur; it was the first use of this fabric in a Steiff toy. The bear was also the company's first stuffed toy with movable joints: it could sit, raise its arms, and turn its head.

The Steiff bear went into production in 1902. The following year, an American importer placed an order for three thousand of the stuffed bears. In 1907, after toy bears became linked with the name of Teddy Roosevelt, American sales of Steiff bears jumped to one million. The success of the company was assured.

Almost from the start, Steiff toys were copied by other manufacturers. Consequently, since 1905, the company has attached a small metal trademark button to each toy. Originally of nickel-plated iron, the button has been made of brass since 1968. Thus for collectors, the Steiff button serves as a toy's pedigree and can sometimes reveal its age.

Made of plush and felt, the vintage Steiff toys at left include some of the company's most appealing animals: the monkey, lobster, and billy goat, as well as the teddy bear.

Owners of a farm and a farm-equipment business in the heart of America's corn belt, the Illinois couple whose corn collectibles are shown here find old farm tools and advertising art to be a natural interest. Over the past twenty-five years they have amassed nearly five hundred items related to growing and processing popcorn and field corn. (Unlike sweet corn, which is grown only for human consumption, field corn is used as livestock feed, and for products like cornmeal and corn oil.)

The memorabilia at right include signs for the Pfister and Dekalb seed companies dating from the first half of the 1900s. "A farmer would post

signs around his field so that anyone passing by would know it was Dekalb corn—or whatever other brand—that they saw growing there," the collectors explain. The painting is by an itinerant artist named Alfred Montgomery who was well known to midwestern farmers in the late 1800s; his primary subject was ears of corn.

The tools in the collection, both handcrafted and factory-made, date from about 1850 to 1930, when most corn processing was done by hand. The corn driers above were used only for "select" ears, those with perfect kernels reserved for seed. The ears were individually dried and the kernels carefully removed by hand.

Continued

Used specifically for seed corn, 19th-century corn driers like those above were designed to hold

individual ears without damaging the kernels. The rings on the drier in the center expand.

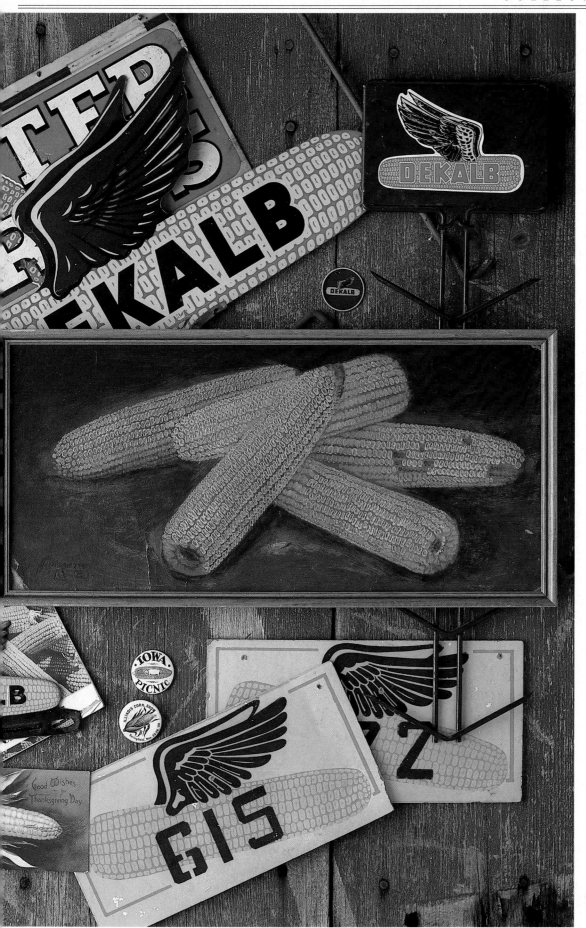

Corn
Collectibles

The corn memorabilia at left
include advertising signs
from the mid-1900s, lapel
buttons, a greeting card, and
a circa 1900 painting by an
itinerant artist named Alfred
Montgomery from Blooming-
ton, Illinois. The corn drier
topped by the sign featuring
a winged ear of Dekalb-
brand corn was made in
the 1970s as a reminder
of an earlier age
of farming.

161

The husking pegs above date from about 1850 to the 1930s. Handmade examples were typically fitted with a leather thong that was slipped around a finger.

The husking pegs, or spikers, above were used to remove the shucks from corn before the ears were brought in from the field. "Everyone had his own idea of what type of tool worked best, and therefore often made his own," note the collectors, who own a variety of hand-carved wooden husking pegs, including several made of bone and one carved from an antler. The two cast-iron pegs, made with a ring to accommodate one finger, were manufactured. The brass example, designed to fit two fingers, was also factory-made.

Once the corn had been shucked it was tossed into a horse-drawn wagon and taken to the barn or silo for storage. (The exceptions were the few select ears that the farmer would tuck into his pocket or under the wagon seat, to be set aside for seed.) After the corn had dried, the kernels

were removed from the ears with corn shellers, which were made in numerous designs.

This collection includes a large number of mechanical corn shellers as well as over forty hand-held versions like those above. In some, the ears of corn were passed through a toothed ring (the tiniest rings in the shellers with graduated rings were designed to accommodate popcorn ears); in others, the ears were held lightly in clamps, then rocked back and forth until the kernels were loosened. The round shellers with funnel-shaped interiors are known as tippers and butters. These highly specialized tools were fitted over the ends of the select ears in order to remove the dwarfed, misshapen, or oversize kernels that were found at the tips and butts. Those less-than-ideal kernels were never used for planting.

Most of the 19th- and early-20th-century corn shellers above were factory-made. The wooden sheller fitted with small spikes, however, was handcrafted.

The collection at right includes bee boxes, smokers, and related beekeeping equipment used during the 19th century. Designed to hold a honeycomb and live bees, screened boxes like the one on the bottom shelf were used as advertising gimmicks by salesmen for Hoges-Horehound Honey Cough Cure.

Beekeeping Equipment

The owner of this 19th-century beekeeping equipment developed an interest in bees as a young boy. "When I was eleven or twelve, the Boy Scouts offered a new merit badge for beekeeping," he recalls. "It happened that a neighbor had several hives and I became intrigued. I learned what I could at the local nature center and then set up my own hive in our back yard." (He never did get his badge, however.)

His introduction to antique bee paraphernalia came when he accompanied his father to flea markets and antiques shows. "Beekeeping was a popular 19th-century pastime," the collector explains, "and a surprising amount of equipment that was used in that period still exists."

Among the most commonly found items are smokers and bee boxes like those at left. The smokers are made of tin with an attached leather bellows; the smoke from a small fire burning inside was used to confuse bees while the keeper gathered the honey. Bee boxes—usually homemade from wood and glass—allowed keepers to trap wild bees temporarily; the bees were then released so that they could be followed back to their natural hives. Most beekeepers designed their own boxes, some of which have as many as five compartments. Homemade hives also appeared in many forms, including little houses like the one above.

The small house above, which measures about two feet wide, is actually a homemade beehive.

Windows on each side allowed the beekeeper to observe the honey-making process.

Patriotic
Costumes

Between the 1876 Centennial and World War I, patriotic zeal ran high in America. The character of Uncle Sam clad in a star-spangled suit and top hat had evolved in political cartoons after the War of 1812; the Statue of Liberty was erected in New York Har-

bor in 1886. Both figures caught the public's imagination.

"During that period, the Fourth of July was a big, big event," says the collector of the patriotic costumes shown here. "There was a parade on every street corner. Adults and children dressed

The patriotic costumes at left date from the 1880s to about 1915, and include both handmade and store-bought items. Manufactured accessories include parasols, handkerchiefs, and scarves.

up and marched as Uncle Sam and Miss Liberty; people even dressed up their pets."

The outfits these patriots wore included those both handmade and store-bought. "They are all surprisingly well made, but after all, they were meant to be used year after year," says the col-lector, who searches for vintage costumes at estate sales and auctions, and often finds Uncle Sam suits complete with their original horsehair beards. He likes to display the costumes throughout his house. "Everyone smiles when they see them," he says.

Selected Reading

Albert, Lillian Smith, and Jane Ford Adams. *The Button Sampler*. New York: Grammercy Publishing, 1951.

Bacot, H. Parrott. *Nineteenth Century Lighting*. West Chester, Pa.: Schiffer Publishing, 1987.

Bishop, Robert, and Judith Reiter Weissman. *Folk Art*. The Knopf Collectors' Guides to American Antiques. New York: Alfred A. Knopf, 1983.

Brett, Vanessa. *Phaidon Guide to Pewter*. Englewood Cliffs, N.J.: Prentice-Hall, 1983.

Carlisle, Lilian Baker. *Hat Boxes and Bandboxes at Shelburne Museum*. Shelburne, Vt.: The Shelburne Museum, 1960.

Cooke, Lawrence S., ed. *Lighting in America*. New York: Universe Books, 1972.

Coysh, A. W., and R. K. Henrywood. *The Dictionary of Blue and White Printed Pottery 1780-1880*. Suffolk, Eng.: The Antique Collectors' Club, 1982.

Franklin, Linda Campbell. *From Hearth to Cookstove*. Florence, Ala.: House of Collectibles, 1976.

Gould, Mary Earle. *Early American Wooden Ware and Other Kitchen Utensils*. Rutland, Vt.: Charles E. Tuttle Company, 1979.

Groves, Sylvia. *The History of Needlework Tools*. New York: Arco Publishing, 1973.

Kebabian, Paul B., and Dudley Witney. *American Woodworking Tools*. Boston: New York Graphic Society, 1978.

Ketchum, William C., Jr. *American Country Pottery: Yellowware and Spongeware*. New York: Alfred A. Knopf, 1987.

Kindig, Paul E. *Butter Prints and Molds*. West Chester, Pa.: Schiffer Publishing, 1986.

Larsen, Ellouise Baker. *American Historical Views on Staffordshire China*. New York: Dover Publications, 1975.

Little, Nina Fletcher. *Neat and Tidy*. New York: E. P. Dutton, 1980.

Lord, Priscilla Sawyer, and Daniel J. Foley. *The Folk Arts and Crafts of New England*. Radnor, Pa.. Chilton Book Company, 1975.

Mayhew, Edgar deN., and Minor Myers, Jr. *A Documentary History of American Interiors from the Colonial Era to 1915*. New York: Charles Scribner's Sons, 1980.

McKearin, Helen. *American Bottles and Flasks*. New York: Crown Publishers, 1978.

Montgomery, Charles F. *A History of American Pewter*. New York: Praeger Publishers, 1973.

Seeler, Katherine and Edgar. *Nantucket Lightship Baskets*. Nantucket, Mass.: The Deermouse Press, 1972.

Seymour, John. *Forgotten Household Crafts*. New York: Alfred A. Knopf, 1987.

Schiffer, Herbert, Peter, and Nancy. *China for America*. West Chester, Pa.: Schiffer Publishing, 1980.

Schiffer, Herbert.F. *The Mirror Book*. West Chester, Pa.: Schiffer Publishing, 1983.

Spargo, John. *The Potters and Potteries of Bennington*. Southampton, N.Y.: Cracker Barrel Press, 1926. Reprint available from the Bennington Museum, Bennington, Vt.

Spillman, Jane Shadel. *American and European Pressed Glass*. Corning, N.Y.: The Corning Museum of Glass, 1981.

Sprigg, June, and David Larkin. *Shaker: Life, Work, and Art*. New York: Stewart, Tabori & Chang, 1987.

Staff, Frank. *The Valentine & Its Origins*. New York: Frederick A. Praeger, 1969.

Stein, Kurt. *Canes & Walking Sticks*. York, Pa.: Liberty Cap Books, 1974.

Thornton, Don. *The Eggbeater Book*. New York: Arbor House, 1983.

Turnbaugh, Sarah Peabody, and William A. Turnbaugh. *Indian Baskets*. West Chester, Pa.: Schiffer Publishing,1986.

Webster, Donald Blake. *Decorated Stoneware Pottery of North America*. Rutland, Vt.: Charles E. Tuttle Company, 1971.

Whiting, Gertrude. *Old-Time Tools and Toys of Needlework*. New York: Dover Publications, 1971.

Photography Credits

Cover and pages 11, 14-15, 20-21, 34, 35, 36 (right), 37, 38, 39, 40, 41, 42-43, 52, 53, 62, 63, 64, 65, 66-67, 70-71, 74-75, 78-79, 80, 82, 83, 90-91, 100, 101 (far right), 102, 103 (except far left), 114, 115, 116, 117, 142-143, 144, 145, 158-159: Steven Mays. Frontispiece and pages 8, 10, 13, 16, 17, 18, 19, 22-23, 24, 26, 27, 28, 29, 36 (left), 48, 49, 50, 54, 55, 58, 59, 60, 61, 68-69, 72, 73, 76-77, 86, 87, 88, 89, 92, 93, 94, 96, 97, 98, 99, 101 (except far right), 104, 105, 106, 108, 109, 110, 112-113, 118, 120, 122-123, 125, 130, 131, 132, 133, 134-135, 136, 137, 138, 139, 140, 141, 150-151, 152, 154, 155, 156, 160, 161, 162, 163, 164, 165: George Ross. Page 12: John Williams Creative Studio, Richardson, TX. Pages 30-31, 44, 45, 46, 47, 128, 129, 146-147, 148, 149, 166-167: Stephen Donelian. Pages 32, 33: all photos ©1986 by Michael Freeman from *Shaker: Life, Work, and Art* by June Sprigg and David Larkin, published by Stewart, Tabori & Chang. By permission of the publisher. Pages 56-57 (top row, left to right): Bettmann Archive, NYC; Bettmann Archive; Schwenkfelder Library, Pennsburg, PA; U.S. Department of Agriculture; Schwenkfelder Library; (bottom row): Bettmann Archive, except third from right, Culver Pictures, NYC. Page 84: New York Historical Society. Pages 85, 107: illustrations by Dolores R. Santoliquido. Page 103 (far left): courtesy Henry Francis duPont Winterthur Museum, Winterthur, DE. Page 121: Jon Elliott. Pages 124, 126, 127: Shelburne Museum, Shelburne, VT.

Prop Credits

The Editors would like to thank the following for their courtesy in lending items for photography. Items not listed below are privately owned. **Page 12**: North American Indian baskets—Leonard Mora, Cameron Trading Post, Cameron, AZ. **Pages 14-15**: Nantucket lightship baskets—from the collection of Nina Hellman, Katonah, NY, and Four Winds Craft Guild, Inc., Nantucket, MA. **Pages 16-17**: wood paneling—Art & Peggy Pappas Antiques, Woodbury, CT. **Pages 20-21**: beeswax candles—Illuminée du Monde, Bristol, VT; votives and pillars—Colonial Candle of Cape Cod, Hyannis, MA; all other candles—Candlewick, Inc., Portland, MI; handmade tiered sconce and freestanding sconce—David Wesley, Columbia, CT; hand-wrought iron hooks and candle snuffer—Historic Housefitters Co., Brewster, NY. **Pages 22-23**: wallcovering, "Shooting Stars," lacquer, from *Winterthur*, vol. 1—Stroheim & Romann, Long Island City, NY. **Page 26**: wood paneling—Art & Peggy Pappas Antiques, Woodbury, CT. **Pages 28-29**: laundry tools—from the collection of Phyllis and James Moffet, Modesto, IL. **Pages 30-31**: wallcovering, "Peterpoint," negative, from *Victoria Morland's A Farmhouse in Provence*—Raintree Designs, NYC. **Pages 38-41**: buttons—Tender Buttons, NYC. **Pages 42-43**: button collages—Tender Buttons, NYC. **Pages 44-47**: tools—from the collection of Daniel Semel, NYC. **Page 54**: buttermaking tools—from the collection of Phyllis and James Moffet, Modesto, IL. **Pages 58-59**: eggbeaters and apple parers—from the collection of Phyllis and James Moffet, Modesto, IL. **Pages 64-65**: ice cream and chocolate molds—Dad's Follies, Winchester, MA. **Pages 66-67**: redware pottery—Bennington Museum, Bennington, VT. **Pages 70-71**: stoneware pottery—Bennington Museum, Bennington, VT. **Pages 72-73**: Rockingham pottery—Houston Museum, Chattanooga, TN. **Pages 74-75**: Bennington pottery—Bennington Museum, Bennington, VT. **Pages 86-87**: Staffordshire and lusterware pottery—Houston Museum, Chattanooga, TN. **Pages 90-91**: Chinese export articles: porcelain pieces (excluding all-blue-and-white Canton plate in front of tea caddy), watercolor painting, inlaid hardwood tea caddy—The Chinese Export Porcelain Co., NYC; French silk brocade with gold threads (on table)—Vito Giallo Antiques, NYC; wallcovering, "Richard Morris Hunt"—Hinson & Co., NYC. **Pages 92-94**: majolica and Toby jugs—Houston Museum, Chattanooga, TN. **Pages 97-99**: spatterware and children's mugs and plates—Houston Museum, Chattanooga, TN. **Pages 100-103**: ceramics consultant—Ellen Paul Denker; agateware teapot and spongeware cow creamer—Leo Kaplan Ltd., NYC; delftware plate, ironstone tureen, majolica dish, Rockingham plate, yellowware bowl—Vito Giallo Antiques, NYC; Flow Blue pitcher and Gaudy Dutch teapot—Houston Museum, Chattanooga, TN; mochaware mug—Bardith Ltd., NYC; sgraffito plate—Henry Francis duPont Winterthur Museum, Winterthur, DE. **Pages 104-110**: all glassware—Houston Museum, Chattanooga, TN. **Pages 112-113**: salt cellars—Rochelle's Antiques, Knoxville, TN. **Pages 114-115**: linens—West River Antiques, Riverdale, NY. **Pages 116-117**: Fiestaware, Harlequinware, LuRay—Helene Guarnaccia Antiques and Collectibles, Fairfield, CT. **Pages 128-129**: wallcovering, "Otis Damask"—Society for the Preservation of New England Antiquities, reproduction—Brunschwig & Fils, NYC; tiles—Country Floors, NYC; loofa sponge, soap, comb and brush—Crabtree & Evelyn; towels—Le Jacquard Français from Palais Royal, Charlottesville,

VA. **Pages 130-135**: shaving mugs, barber bottles, flasks, humidors—Houston Museum, Chattanooga, TN. **Pages 138-141**: desk boxes, pens, paper clips, inkwells—Coleman & May Antiques and Decorative Arts, Washington, D.C. **Page 141**: linens—Regina Sugrue, Riverdale, NY. **Pages 144-145**: archival photo album, ephemera storage bags, acid-free thumb-cut paper envelopes, Mylar fold-lock sleeves, brayer, acid-free storage boxes, archival gloves, encapsulation materials—Light Impressions, Rochester, NY; encapsulation instructions adapted from material prepared by the Northeast Document Conservation Center, Andover, MA. **Pages 148-149**: trade cards—from the collections of Kit Barry, Brattleboro, VT, and Joe Rosson, Knoxville, TN. **Pages 158-159**: vintage Steiff animals from the collection of, and available from, Dee Hockenberry and Lorraine Oakley, Albion, NY, and Francis Nichols/The Joy Toy Man, Wilmington, NC; rag rug—ABC International Design Rugs, NYC; wallcovering, "Spring Daisy" #686-GC6185, from *The Country Manor*—Gear, NYC. **Pages 160-163**: corn tools—from the collection of Phyllis and James Moffet, Modesto, IL. **Pages 166-167**: Uncle Sam and Miss Liberty costumes—from the collection of Allan Katz, Woodbridge, CT; Shaker pegs and hangers—Shaker Workshops, Concord, MA.

Index

Acknowledgments

Our thanks to Judy and Alex Awrylo, Bunny and Kent and Beachler, the Bennington Museum, Pat Briggs, Charles Browne, Lois Carey, Jimmy Cramer, Ellie Cullman, Ellen Paul Denker, Jeannine and Otto Dobbs, Diana Epstein, Kathy Epstein, Vito Giallo, Heather and Wayne Graf, Jean Gross, Helene Guarnaccia, Margaret and Charles Gure, Loretta Hanes, Claudia and Carroll Hopf, Alda Horner, the Houston Museum, Susan and Stephen Hunkins, Dennis Inch, Rebecca Jones, Ruth Kaplan, Allan Katz, William Lewan, Laura Luckey, Ruth S. Mann, George H. Meyer, George H. Meyer, Jr., Phyllis and James Moffet, Howard Monroe, Barbara and Charles Randau, Frances Beck Reynolds, Roy Rochelle, Millicent Safro, David Schorsch, Dona and Fred Schuller, Daniel Semel, Patricia Smith, Regina Sugrue, Noreen and Carl Thoresen, Jessie and Jeremy Ulin, Angela Usrey, Ed Weaver, Holly and David Wesley, David Wright, Cathie Zusy.

First printing
Published simultaneously in Canada
School and library distribution by Silver Burdett Company,
Morristown, New Jersey

TIME-LIFE is a trademark of Time Incorporated U.S.A.

Production by Giga Communications, Inc.
Printed in U.S.A.

Library of Congress Cataloging-in-Publication Data

Country collections.
p.cm. — (American country)
Includes index.
ISBN 0-8094-6783-6. — ISBN 0-8094-6784-4 (lib. bdg.)
1. Country life—United States—Collectibles.
2. Decorative arts—United States
I. Time-Life Books. II. Series.
NK805.C686   1989
745.1'0973'075—dc19   89-4370
CIP

American Country was created by Rebus, Inc., and published by Time-Life Books.

REBUS, INC.

Publisher: RODNEY FRIEDMAN • Editor: MARYA DALRYMPLE
Executive Editor: RACHEL D. CARLEY • Managing Editor: BRENDA SAVARD • Consulting Editor: CHARLES L. MEE, JR.
Associate Editor: SARA COLLINS MEDINA • Copy Editor: HELEN SCOTT-HARMAN
Writers: JUDITH CRESSY, ROSEMARY G. RENNICKE • Freelance Writers: JOE L. ROSSON, MARY SEARS
Design Editors: NANCY MERNIT, CATHRYN SCHWING
Test Kitchen Director: GRACE YOUNG • Editor, The Country Letter: BONNIE J. SLOTNICK
Editorial Assistant: SANTHA CASSELL • Contributing Editors: ANNE MOFFAT, DEE SHAPIRO
Indexer: MARILYN FLAIG

Art Director: JUDITH HENRY • Associate Art Director: SARA REYNOLDS
Designers: AMY BERNIKER, TIMOTHY JEFFS
Photographer: STEVEN MAYS • Photo Editor: SUE ISRAEL
Photo Assistant: ROB WHITCOMB • Freelance Photographers: STEPHEN DONELIAN,
JON ELLIOTT, GEORGE ROSS • Freelance Photo Stylist: VALORIE FISHER

Series Consultants: BOB CAHN, HELAINE W. FENDELMAN, LINDA C. FRANKLIN, GLORIA GALE,
KATHLEEN EAGEN JOHNSON, JUNE SPRIGG, CLAIRE WHITCOMB

Time-Life Books Inc. is a wholly owned subsidiary of TIME INCORPORATED.

FOUNDER: HENRY R. LUCE 1898-1967

Editor-in-Chief: JASON McMANUS • Chairman and Chief Executive Officer: J. RICHARD MUNRO
President and Chief Operating Officer: N. J. NICHOLAS JR. • Editorial Director: RICHARD B. STOLLEY
Executive Vice President, Books: KELSO F. SUTTON • Vice President, Books: PAUL V. McLAUGHLIN

TIME-LIFE BOOKS INC.

Editor: GEORGE CONSTABLE • Executive Editor: ELLEN PHILLIPS
Director of Design: LOUIS KLEIN • Director of Editorial Resources: PHYLLIS K. WISE
Editorial Board: RUSSELL B. ADAMS JR., DALE M. BROWN, ROBERTA CONLAN, THOMAS H. FLAHERTY,
LEE HASSIG, DONIA ANN STEELE, ROSALIND STUBENBERG
Director of Photography and Research: JOHN CONRAD WEISER
Assistant Director of Editorial Resources: ELISE RITTER GIBSON

President: CHRISTOPHER T. LINEN • Chief Operating Officer: JOHN M. FAHEY JR.
Senior Vice Presidents: ROBERT M. DeSENA, JAMES L. MERCER, PAUL R. STEWART
Vice Presidents: STEPHEN L. BAIR, RALPH J. CUOMO, NEAL GOFF, STEPHEN L. GOLDSTEIN,
JUANITA T. JAMES, CAROL KAPLAN, SUSAN J. MARUYAMA, ROBERT H. SMITH, JOSEPH J. WARD
Director of Production Services: ROBERT J. PASSANTINO
Supervisor of Quality Control: JAMES KING

For information about any Time-Life book please call 1-800-621-7026, or write:
Reader Information, Time-Life Customer Service
P.O. Box C-32068, Richmond, Virginia 23261-2068

Time-Life Books Inc. offers a wide range of fine recordings, including a Rock 'n' Roll Era series.
For subscription information, call 1-800-621-7026, or write TIME-LIFE MUSIC,
P.O. Box C-32068, Richmond, Virginia 23261-2068.